W9-ASK-790

The
Secretary
Grid®

The Secretary Grid®

Robert R. Blake
Jane Srygley Mouton
Artie Stockton

amacom

American Management Associations

Library of Congress Cataloging in Publication Data

Blake, Robert Rogers, 1918-
    The secretary grid.

    Includes index.
    1. Secretaries. I. Mouton, Jane Srygley.
II. Stockton, Artie.   III. Title
HF5547.5.B56   1983   651.3'741   82-73514
ISBN 0-8144-5762-2

First Printing

Preface

Few working relationships provide greater opportunity for teamwork than that between a boss and a secretary, and few provide greater satisfaction than that derived from effective teamwork of this kind.

Teamwork doesn't just happen, however. A lot of thought and analysis must go into what it is and what it is not. Teamwork is possible only when agreement exists between boss and secretary as to how best to serve the overall interests of the organization.

Grid theory is used to aid the development of teamwork. It was created by Blake and Mouton in 1964 and was originally used as a framework for basic theories about managerial effectiveness. Grid concepts have proved valuable in many other areas as well, including sales, supervision, education, nursing, academic administration, and social work.

The Secretary Grid distinguishes between effective and ineffective ways in which secretaries interact with their bosses and others. It encourages secretaries to assess their own characteristic style and to consider what changes they need to make to become more effective. Then both secretary and boss can learn the concepts, the work practices, and the specific skills on which effective teamwork is built.

In addition to operating the office support system, secretaries are sometimes asked to exercise responsibility and leadership in other areas—for example, attending meetings on substantive issues as a representative of the boss and working with the boss's subordinates to develop a budget. These kinds of responsibilities

v

are often delegated to executive secretaries or administrative assistants. In this book we have concentrated on the more basic tasks that secretaries perform in maintaining the office support system.

We recognize that the number of male secretaries and female managers is increasing steadily in the typical U.S. corporation today. To make reading easier, however, we have referred to the secretary as *she* and the boss as *he* throughout, rather than using cumbersome *he or she* constructions.

Robert R. Blake
Jane Srygley Mouton
Artie Stockton

Contents

The
Secretary
Grid®

1
The Secretary's Role

Few executives or managers are complete without a secretary. She provides indispensable support: typing, taking dictation, answering and placing calls, greeting visitors, keeping files, maintaining an appointment schedule, and making plane reservations. More important, she often knows a great deal about management, finance, and current events in the business world generally. She may have special skills as a legal secretary, a medical secretary, or a technical secretary. More than likely, she knows the intricate workings of the organization. Indeed, more than one secretary has trained a series of bosses as they have come and gone. She is a professional in her own right who has a decisive influence on the success of her boss and the company.

An accurate description?

Yes, as far as it goes, but it just scratches the surface. When you think about it, a secretary's contributions are far more extensive than those just described. Let's examine the job more closely.

Office Climate

Every office has a climate, and it has nothing to do with air conditioning. This climate comes through in the tempo of activities and the ways in which things get done. It is seen in office housekeeping, but not of the janitorial kind. It comes through in whether papers are stacked or whether there is an orderly arrangement of files. It is influenced by office decor—pictures, carpet, drapes, and so on. Sound, too, is a factor. The atmosphere may be quiet and purposeful, or noisy and disruptive, with people shouting, typewriters clattering, and the persistent ringing of telephones.

Office climate is measured in conversations overheard between the boss and the secretary, in the secretary's conversations on the phone, and in the way the secretary meets and greets visitors. Climate can be frenetic, friendly, artificial, professional, or dead. You may think that all this is of no great importance. Climate, however, has a profound influence on how well (or how poorly) things get done. The climate may be so warm and friendly that the office becomes a gathering place—a social center for conversations having nothing to do with business. Or it may be so oppressive that even those whose presence may be desirable or necessary say, "I hate to go to the twelfth floor; it's so stiff and formal."

The boss influences office climate by the manner in which he conducts business. In many respects, though, the secretary's role in climate setting has more impact, because, in many business matters, even the boss may take a cue from her. Many of the factors that help create the climate are directly affected by the secretary's approach to things. Therefore, it is the rare secretary who cannot influence climate.

Consider the matter of operational housekeeping. The activities that are part of operating a support system range from researching the files for background information to having replacement batteries on hand for dictation equipment. Many of these duties are far from glamorous, but they make the difference in whether the boss can concentrate on the tasks that are vital to the organization's success.

One of the paradoxes of the support system the secretary operates is that her contributions are unlikely to be noticed when things go well. They become visible only when things go poorly or when a slip-up occurs.

Secretary-Boss Relationship

The quality of the relationship between the boss and the secretary can play an important role in how effectively work gets done. This relationship can be examined in more depth by studying the secretary's role as a sounding board—a person who has access to privileged information and who contributes to the quality of the boss's thinking and decision making. Another part of the secretary's support of her boss is interacting with others outside the boss-secretary relationship. These interfaces with others include the role of gatekeeping, that is, determining who speaks to or meets with her boss. It also includes speaking for the boss and speaking for others. The secretary also sees that written communication and verbal reporting are effective. Finally, if she manages other people in the organization, she also plays a supervisory role.

Initiative

A secretary deals with many of the same people as her boss, sometimes as an intermediary, sometimes concurrently. Whatever her sources of information, she, like any executive or manager, needs to be aware of the importance of acquiring thorough and accurate information. This is done by inquiring. Through discreet inquiries, she may unearth much information that would not otherwise come to light. She may notice discrepancies and contradictions where the data just do not fit conclusions being reached. She can inquire into deeper meanings and wider interpretations of a report and keep the boss from making an error. This is truly a great skill, and if the secretary does possess it, she adds a second set of eyes and ears to her boss's understanding of problems and situations. When this is done well, she can inquire without polarizing, seek information without spying, and test assumptions without provoking defensiveness.

Sounding Board

Every executive or manager has someone against whom ideas can be tested, thinking can be subjected to critical analysis, and possible actions can be considered and evaluated. This person may be a colleague in the corporation, a spouse, a lawyer, or, very frequently, a secretary. Performance of this sounding board function is one of the critical aspects of a secretary's effectiveness. In acting as a sounding board, the secretary does not simply sit and listen and then make suggestions. Rather, she listens, reflects, questions, and points out implications the boss may not be aware of. In doing this, she provides a form of support.

Similarly, a secretary often plays a critical role as a confidante. Secretaries know what is going on; they know the issues that are involved; they know, sometimes as well as the boss, the pros and cons of any given decision. A secretary who can act as a sounding board, and who does so objectively, is an indispensable contributor to her boss's effectiveness.

Privileged Communication

A secretary is a communications nerve center. There are very few matters about which the secretary is uninformed either directly or indirectly. If she does not have firsthand information, she can almost always put two and two together and figure out what is going on. The secretary's position at the center of the information network raises the issue of privileged communication and how best to handle it. Privileged communication is information the secretary is not free to divulge, no matter how helpful it might be to others. And the key to handling it is the answer to the question, "Who owns the information?" The answer is, "The boss does." In other words, it is the boss's to share, to withhold, to edit, to deny, and so on. The secretary's position with regard to this information is that of the hotel desk clerk to the contents of the safety deposit box that stores the guest's valuables. She doesn't own it, but she knows what it is and what is in it. The root of the word *secretary* is, after all, *secret:* "something kept from the knowledge of others."

This may mean that the secretary possesses information that many other people are deeply interested in but that her boss wishes to have kept confidential. Her ability to keep such confidential corporate information *confidential* is a measure of her effectiveness and is greatly appreciated by her boss.

Interfaces

Gatekeeping

Secretaries are decision makers, not in the conventional sense of deciding what alternative or course of action to pursue on a given organizational issue, but, rather, in that they have responsibility for determining who gets in to see the boss and what gets placed on his desk. The secretary also determines whether the input is trivial and a waste of time or whether it is critical and highly significant. She determines what correspondence she can answer and what should be given to the boss and in what priority. She determines what telephone calls are of sufficient urgency to warrant interrupting her boss. In fact, it is the secretary who determines to a very significant degree what information the boss does or does not receive. The boss obviously influences this by his requests, questions, instructions, complaints, and so on, but within these boundaries it is the secretary who exercises the final judgment when every letter cannot be read and every call cannot be answered.

Speaking for the Boss

Many times the boss says, "Would you get in touch with so-and-so and explain the situation? Let me know what he thinks." This is an important assignment. It is part of the support system, but it is by no means a routine task. It means understanding why the boss wants the contact made. It may also mean being able to ask the questions the boss should have asked but didn't.

Speaking for Others

A secretary also acts as a representative of her boss to those outside the office. She is responsible for seeing that others receive information that the boss has asked her to pass on. Indeed, on many occasions when the boss has not given instructions she must decide whether information available to her is to be passed on. It is her job, in other words, to reflect her boss accurately and to interpret him to those he does business with.

The secretary must understand why a person with whom her boss deals responds as he or she does, represent her boss in a professional manner, and give the boss information about her interaction with the other person that conveys its full complexity and subtlety. At a simple level, it means being able to answer questions the boss might ask, such as, "What did he mean by that?" At a more complex level, it means responding accurately and thoughtfully to the question, "Why did she request that?"

The Written Word

Writing skills are important, and the secretary is the most appropriate person to exercise quality control of the written word. Many managers are not the best communicators in the world. When it comes to writing skills, they may express themselves in highly technical, complex, or confusing language, and unless someone can convert their "communication" into something that is thoroughly comprehensible, it simply won't be understood. And if the secretary can't do it, who can? The necessary skills include the editoral ability to take a technically difficult piece of writing and "translate" it into simple language.

Systems Manager

A word may be appropriate here about word processing centers. The current revolution in word processing is reshaping the entire concept of office work. Many word processing centers operate in such a way that they separate the manager, who produces the written word, from those who actually put it into print. For instance, a word processing center organized along the lines of a manufacturing operation reduces to a minimum personal contact between the originator of the word production and the processor of the final document.

This book deals with those aspects of a secretary's job that do not involve word processing except when supervising a word processing center is also part of her task. Thus the issues involved in an effective secretary-boss relationship remain the same, even though the word processing aspects of the secretary's job may add a new dimension to it.*

Supervisory responsibilities, of course, place different and increased demands on a secretary's skills. Managing others means having the ability to achieve results through people in an effective manner. A secretary's managerial responsibilities may extend to only one or two other people, or they may cover a whole department. In her capacity as office manager, she carries out the same managerial functions as her boss—planning, organizing, directing, controlling, and so on.

All secretaries do not operate in the same way, of course. Some seem able to maintain and operate this kind of support system in a marvelously smooth, efficient, and creative manner, while others seem harassed and under intolerable pressure. Others do it in an acceptable way, maintaining a good, steady tempo but without contributing much inspiration or support. For others the office is a second home—a place where visitors are welcome and the boss made comfortable. Then there are secretaries who go through the motions, awaiting day's end, hoping to get by without a calamity occurring. There is also the secretary who dominates, but in such an endearing way that she

---

*T. M. Lodahl and L. K. Williams, "An Opportunity for OD: The Office Revolution," *OD Practitioner*, Vol. 10, No. 4 (1978), pp. 9–11.

practically owns the boss, who in many respects has become her dependent.

Secretarial functions, then, are carried out in different ways. Through Grid theory we can examine how different secretaries fulfill their responsibilities and evaluate the consequences of each style, both from the standpoint of the secretary's own effectiveness and from the standpoint of the extent to which the support system she creates truly benefits the organization. Then we will be in a position to evaluate better and poorer ways of operating this highly important support system and to identify the skills a secretary needs to make the maximum contribution to her boss's success and to the effectiveness of the organization.

Plan of the Book

The manner in which the secretary manages her relationships with others reflects her dominant and backup Grid styles. Each style—9,1; 1,9; 1,1; 5,5; 9,9, and maternalism—will be described in its own chapter. Several different aspects of secretarial work are described to show how a secretary operates within any given Grid style.

First is the matter of creating a positive office climate, one that makes visitors feel welcome and that permits the boss and others to engage in deliberation, maintaining their concentration because interruptions are kept to a minimum. Next is the one-to-one working relationship between a secretary and her boss. One of the most important aspects of this relationship is her role as sounding board and confidante. The way she listens, reflects, questions, and probes can help to determine whether his consideration of a problem is superficial or thorough. Her functioning in this role can make a difference between good, indifferent, or poor decision making on the boss's part. Next there is the matter of the secretary as a gatekeeper, being constantly aware of the importance of admitting everyone who needs to see the boss as well as ensuring that he gets every call and piece of correspondence he needs. This role also involves keeping time-wasting contacts, calls, and correspondence to a minimum. To do this effectively, the secretary has to know a great deal about her boss's business, not only in general terms but also quite frequently in technical terms so she can evaluate and order according to their importance a host of complex and subtle matters. These are some of the skills necessary for effective teamwork.

We will also examine the secretary's responsibility as a systems manager. How she works with and through those she supervises determines the quantity and quality of productivity she is able to contribute to the organization.

Those who are just beginning a secretarial career might read Chapter 9 first. It details the nuts and bolts of being a secretary—opening the mail, proper use of the telephone, greeting visitors, managing time, filing, and so on. This chapter is also a good refresher for experienced secretaries.

A significant aspect of Chapter 10 is that it answers a secretary's question, "Now that I understand myself better, what about my boss?" It presents numerous examples of secretary-boss situations and allows readers to test their understanding of Grid concepts, from the point of view of both the secretary's Grid style and the boss's.

All of this is basic for thinking through the implications for self-development discussed in the final chapter. The appendix (which includes a selected bibliography) deals with some more technical aspects of Grid theory. It too can enrich the study of the Grid by those wishing to examine it in greater depth.

2
The Secretary Grid

Some understanding of Grid theories as they apply to the secretary is essential if we are to come to grips with the issues discussed in Chapter 1. Grid concepts and theories, as described in *The New Managerial Grid* (Gulf, 1978), have been widely applied to selling, to supervisory work, and so on, and many secretaries may already be acquainted with them, at least in a general way.

As used in this book the Grid provides secretaries with a way of learning more about themselves. It permits them to study a series of different strategies that they can use in carrying out their jobs rather than giving them a recipe for the "one best way." In this manner the Grid helps secretaries sort out the alternatives available and weigh the strengths and weaknesses of each.

As a secretary goes about her work, she has two major concerns. The first is for the task at hand (production or results)—those activities essential for supporting the administrative or managerial level where she is employed. Whether she is a secretary to one or several managers, it means the way she manages her activities with and through people—such as handling mail and correspondence, preparing reports, and setting up travel itineraries—as well as being a sounding board, speaking for her boss, speaking for others, and so on.

The second concern is for those with whom she is in contact as she carries out her secretarial duties. These include her boss, the other members of the organization with whom her boss deals, administrative superiors, her subordinates, and people with whom she interacts in other departments within the organization and outside it—as they affect the performance of her own activities.

These two concerns come together in many ways, and the specific manner in which these two concerns mesh determines a secretary's style. Concern for the task and concern for others are revealed in vastly different ways. A high concern for production coupled with a low concern for others and a low concern for production coupled with a high concern for others are significantly different. And both of these differ from a high concern for others that is joined with an equally high concern for productivity.

The Secretary Grid® appears in Figure 1. The horizontal axis indicates concern for production, the vertical axis, concern for others. Each has a 9-point scale, with 1 representing a minimum concern, 5 representing an intermediate degree of concern, and 9 representing maximum concern. Eighty-one possible combinations are represented on the Grid. Each of these 81 positions represents a theory about how the secretary goes about accomplishing her task with and through others. Theory is a valuable tool for helping the secretary see the assumptions on which her behavior is based. The various theories are important because they help a secretary understand her own behavior as well as the reactions of those she deals with. With a sound understanding of her own behavior, the secretary can strive for excellence in performing her own job and in helping others to do their best in their jobs.

Going Around the Grid

The main emphasis here is on the theories in the corners and in the middle of the Grid. These theories are the most distinctive. They are the ones seen most often in day-to-day circumstances. No doubt, as you consider each Grid style, someone you know will come to mind as an example of that particular style.

Figure 1. The Secretary Grid®

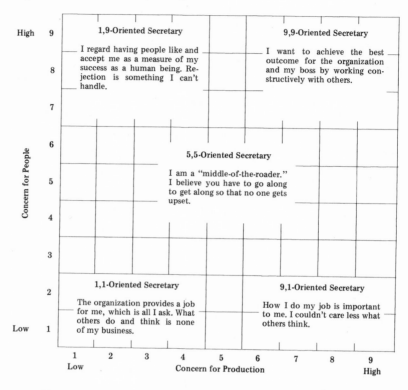

In the lower right corner is the style of a 9,1-oriented secretary. Her high concern (9) for performing the task is coupled with little or no concern (1) for others as individuals with thoughts and feelings. Secretly, she may be called "battle-ax" or some even less flattering nickname.

In the upper left corner of the Grid is the 1,9-oriented secretary, who joins minimum concern for the task with maximum concern for others. She wants to develop friendly relations with people. She hopes they will respond to her warmth and friendliness and accept her. She exudes "sweetness and light."

What others think of her and what they want from her come first; things or outcomes have little importance.

In the lower left corner, the 1,1-oriented secretary is characterized by uninvolvement. You might think of her as a department store mannequin. She is functional but exhibits no personality. She has little concern for her job or people. You may wonder how a person with this orientation can keep her job. Think about it. Many secretaries merely function, but for whatever reason, they have mentally walked out, no longer feeling the enthusiasm they once had. As long as the paycheck comes they hang on, doing the required, just enough to get by and no more.

The secretary with a 5,5 orientation, the Grid style in the center, uses middle-of-the-road tactics. This secretary wants to be sure of her popularity. After everyone has had a say, she jumps in on the side of the majority. She may keep her feelings from being too visible, and she always knows which side is politically safe. Some might call her the "secretary-crat."

In the upper right corner is the 9,9-oriented secretary. She knows that a high concern for results and a high concern for people are two sides of the same coin. The secretary with this orientation performs her own tasks well and gains the involvement, participation, and commitment of others in achieving the highest possible results in terms of quality, quantity, and personal satisfaction. She is known as a real "star."

Dominant and Backup Grid Styles

A secretary's Grid style is usually consistent over a range of situations, but it is also true that people sometimes shift from one Grid style to another. How can a person shift and change if most of us have one dominant set of Grid assumptions? The answer is that not only do most secretaries have a dominant Grid style, they also have a backup style; sometimes even a second, third, or fourth backup style. A secretary's backup style becomes active when it is difficult or impossible for her to use her dominant or most characteristic Grid style. It is the style reverted to when she is experiencing pressure, tension, strain, or frustration, or is in situations of conflict that she cannot solve in her most characteristic way.

Relationships between dominant and backup styles can be seen quite easily. How parents deal with their children is a good example. First, parents may try problem solving in a 9,9-oriented way. When this does not work, they may get tough and even add a touch of ridicule—9,1-oriented ways of trying to get the child's attention and compliance. Then, when resentment and rejection have been created without producing a successful outcome, parents may switch to expressions of love and kindness and hope that a 1,9 attitude will bring the child around. Still unable to elicit cooperation, they may either return to a 9,1 strategy of threat and punishment or throw up their hands in a 1,1 way and say, "I give up."

There appear to be few, if any, strong natural or preferred links between any one Grid style as dominant and any other as backup. The great array of possible dominant-backup combinations is what makes individuals unique. The point is that Grid styles are not fixed and unchanging; each of us may shift as the situation changes.

Assumptions and Grid Styles

Each Grid style is based on a set of basic assumptions from which people deal with one another. An assumption is what a person takes for granted as being a true or reliable basis for action. People do not often question their basic assumptions. If you, as a secretary, were to deal with others without making assumptions, you would have no consistency at all. Your behavior would be haphazard.

Even so, it is not enough to have just any set of assumptions, because some assumptions are sound and some are unsound.

Getting to know what your own assumptions are will permit you to check out your approaches to managing tasks and dealing with people and to examine alternative assumptions that might make you more effective. Learning the Grid framework will increase your understanding of what kinds of actions are likely to lead to certain kinds of results. It too can help you examine alternative assumptions and how these undergird the different ways of behaving.

The emphasis is on self-understanding. Once you know more about your dominant and backup Grid styles through examining the next several chapters, we will return to the question, "How can I change my Grid style to increase my secretarial effectiveness?"

In the following set of self-evaluation questions, six elements are used to provide descriptions through which you can identify your Grid assumptions. These elements are Decisions, Convictions, Conflict, Emotions, Thoroughness, and Enthusiasm. Six sentences are provided under each element. Consider each sentence as a possible description of yourself. Place a 6 beside the sentence you think is most like yourself—the actual you, not the ideal you. One of the barriers to describing yourself accurately is self-deception, so be as objective as you can. Self-deception means you picture the *best* you, not the *real* you as known by other people. In other words, here you are asked to describe the person you are now.

Place a 5 beside the sentence you think is next most like yourself. Continue ranking the other sentences down to a 1 for the sentence least characteristic of you. There can be no ties.

Element 1: Decisions

_____   A1. I accept the decisions of others with indifference.
_____   B1. I support decisions that promote good relations.
_____   C1. I search for workable, even though not perfect, decisions.

_____   D1. I expect decisions I make to be treated as final.

_____   E1. I have the final say but make a sincere effort to see that my decisions are accepted.

_____   F1. I place high value on getting sound creative decisions that result in understanding and agreement.

Element 2: Convictions

_____   A2. I avoid taking sides by not revealing my opinions, attitudes, and ideas.

_____   B2. I embrace opinions, attitudes, and ideas of others rather than pushing my own.

_____   C2. When others hold ideas, opinions, or attitudes different from my own, I try to meet them halfway.

_____   D2. I stand up for my ideas, opinions, and attitudes, even though it sometimes results in upsetting people.

_____   E2. I maintain strong convictions but permit others to express ideas different from my own so that they sense my concern.

_____   F2. I listen for and seek out ideas, opinions, and attitudes different from my own. I have clear convictions but respond to ideas sounder than my own by changing my mind.

Element 3: Conflict

_____   A3. When conflict arises, I prefer to remain neutral.

_____   B3. I try to avoid generating conflict; but when it does appear, I try to soothe feelings to keep people together.

_____   C3. When conflict arises, I try to find fair solutions that accommodate others.

_____   D3. When conflict arises, I try to cut it off or to win my position.

_____ E3. When conflict arises, I terminate it but thank people for expressing their views.

_____ F3. When conflict arises, I try to identify and resolve the underlying problems that are causing it.

Element 4: Emotions

_____ A4. By remaining uninvolved, I rarely get stirred up.

_____ B4. Because of the disapproval tensions can produce, I react in a warm and friendly way.

_____ C4. Under tension, I feel unsure and anxious about how to meet others' expectations.

_____ D4. When things are not going right, I defend, resist, and come back with counterarguments.

_____ E4. When things do not go right, I express strong disapproval.

_____ F4. When aroused, I reexamine my own and others' motives and assumptions in an effort to achieve a better understanding of the tensions being produced.

Element 5: Thoroughness

_____ A5. I do as I am told, just enough to get by.

_____ B5. My completion of tasks depends on what others demand of me; others' feelings are what count.

_____ C5. I tend to know enough about my work responsibilities to keep things from piling up, but if I get in a crunch, someone will always bail me out.

_____ D5. I know every aspect of my work responsibilities; no one is going to catch me short.

_____ E5. I take pride in fulfilling my responsibilities, especially since I think others benefit from my example.

_____ F5. I am familiar in detail with every aspect of my

responsibilities and make sure they are fulfilled to a degree I can be proud of.

Element 6: Enthusiasm

_____   A6. I exert enough effort to get by.
_____   B6. I support, encourage, and compliment others on what they want to do.
_____   C6. I offer positive suggestions to keep things moving along.
_____   D6. I drive myself and others.
_____   E6. I stress loyalty and give appreciation to those who support me.
_____   F6. I exert vigorous effort and others join in.

Use Figure 2 to summarize your rankings so you can answer the question, "What Grid style is most typical of me?" Copy your rankings for the Decisions element in row 1, your rankings for

Figure 2. Tally of first self-evaluation rankings on Grid elements.

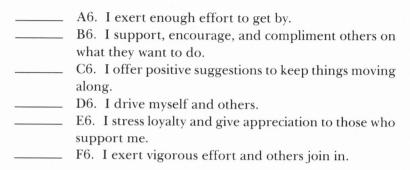

Element	Grid Style					
	1,1	1,9	5,5	9,1	Maternalism	9,9
1. Decisions	A1__	B1__	C1__	D1__	E1_____	F1__
2. Convictions	A2__	B2__	C2__	D2__	E2_____	F2__
3. Conflict	A3__	B3__	C3__	D3__	E3_____	F3__
4. Emotions	A4__	B4__	C4__	D4__	E4_____	F4__
5. Thoroughness	A5__	B5__	C5__	D5__	E5_____	F5__
6. Enthusiasm	A6__	B6__	C6__	D6__	E6_____	F6__
TOTAL	A__	B__	C__	D__	E_____	F__

the Convictions element in row 2, and so on. Then add up the scores in each column.

The highest possible total for any Grid style is 36. This means that you were consistent in picking the same Grid style for all six elements. The Grid style on which you have the highest number is what you see as your dominant style. The one with the next highest is what you see as your backup. The Grid style with the lowest number represents the style that you reject most strongly as representing you. The lowest possible total for any Grid style is 6. This represents the strongest possible rejection of a style.

Remember, this is a self-description. It may not represent the true you, because most of us deceive ourselves in certain ways. However, it is a point of departure to keep in mind as you read the book. After you have a greater understanding of Grid styles and of your own particular approach, rerank yourself.

As demonstrated in numerous research studies and empirical investigations, the six elements presented here are fundamental to a clear understanding of the assumptions that individual secretaries make about their work and about their interactions with others.* The six elements are also a sound basis for understanding the personal characteristics of your boss.

We are now ready for an in-depth study of each Secretary Grid style. In the next six chapters we examine the pure Grid styles. As you read, place yourself in as many of the situations as your possibly can. Imagine what your reactions would be. Then check back and forth to see how your reactions square with the data you developed about yourself in this chapter. Chapter 11 will help you to interpret the rankings you have just completed and to evaluate their implications for your own personal effectiveness as a secretary.

---

*Robert R. Blake and Jane S. Mouton, *The New Managerial Grid* (Houston: Gulf Publishing Company, 1978).

3
The Task-Oriented Secretary
(The 9,1 Orientation)

The 9,1 orientation, shown in the lower right corner of the Grid, couples high concern for task with low concern for people. This type of secretary seeks to dominate others and maintain control over circumstances. She is motivated to win by proving herself smarter, more capable, and more determined, and by yielding to no one. The emphasis is on willpower. This can lead to an inflexible determination to stay in control. The motto is, "You've got to look out for Number 1." Competition is so important that she is likely to say, "When there is no one else to contend with, I compete with myself."

Sometimes she does not get the results she anticipates no matter how hard she tries, and then she feels like a failure. Her greatest fear is of making a mistake or of losing control because someone resists. When she no longer feels in control, she usually places the blame for the problem on something or someone else. Her attitude is, "Next time I'll keep a tighter hold—never depend on anyone but yourself."

When results are satisfying, she feels good, in charge, strong, needing nothing and having little or no appreciation for what others may be contributing.

Office Climate

The 9,1-oriented secretary operates her office as a command post, with the telephone as its nerve center. The "hold" button is

20

the control switch that allows her to do four things simultaneously: greet someone, instruct someone, and answer someone, all while banging away on her typewriter. As a result, others are likely to feel inconvenienced by her priorities. A visitor to the office is reluctant to carry on a conversation with her because of the frequent interruptions. The people with whom she does her boss's business are likely to feel that their needs inconvenience her. Therefore, they keep their contact to a minimum, making their requests or telephone inquiries as short as possible to avoid her anger at their waste of her time.

Looked at from the secretary's side, curtness is her way of telling others what is not okay. For example, "Please get to the point" means "You're wasting my precious time." "You don't need to repeat" means "I got the point the first time." "No use bothering with it" says "I'm not going to waste my time on that one." This command post is no place for small talk or loitering. Its sole function is as a place where you state your business, get it done, salute, and get going.

This secretary's pressure for results may create bedlam, but her work area is usually neatly arranged. In place are all the items that she needs to do her job well and efficiently. The atmosphere says "Hands off." No one dares enter unless invited, nor would anyone remove anything from or place anything on her desk without consulting her. She casts a critical eye on the work areas of others, and in the case of subordinates, her directive is simple: "Clean it up."

The climate resembles that of a battle station. It generates its own brand of politics: the politics of power, win-or-lose, and "to the victor belong the spoils." Secretaries, no less than the managers with whom they work, become entrapped in these battle lines and become active combatants. When the secretary tries to scout out the enemy by gathering vital information that she thinks can reduce the risks of defeat or increase the likelihood of victory, the other side may successfully block her attempts.

The main features of a 9,1-oriented climate within the support system itself are seen in the following:

Grace arrives at work and hurries to her desk. "Good morning," says Natalie, the receptionist.

"Forget the good," snaps Grace. "I have a million things to do today." Natalie doesn't respond but turns quietly to her work. Grace picks up the phone and dials the travel agency. "Jim, this is Grace. Please have those tickets here by ten. They were late last time, remember?" She hangs up after making sure she receives compliance from Jim. A few minutes later she's on the intercom to her boss, making sure he knows she will be ready for dictation soon.

Get the picture? The pressure-cooker aspects of a 9,1-oriented secretary's office are all too obvious. The climate is tense, with cooperation on the outside, resistance beneath the surface. The only choice this secretary has is to exert her will and to control the situation.

Secretary-Boss Relationship

The secretary-boss relationship can be characterized in a number of ways. One thing is clear: The 9,1-oriented secretary is the boss as far as her own responsibilities are concerned. On the positive side, the boss can be sure she will get the job done. On the other hand, her relationships with those she works with will be fragile. There are many bosses who are willing to let their 9,1-oriented secretaries "run the show," either unaware of or choosing to ignore the resentment and frustration her take-charge style creates.

The 9,1-oriented secretary's relationship with the boss reveals much about her Grid style. She is inclined to dominate and control the boss as much as she seeks to dominate others in the office. When she tries to tell her boss who, what, where, when, or how, she often manipulates him, if not directly then indirectly, in ways that make her Grid style obvious. If the boss resists strongly and she fights back, her tenure is likely to be short-lived.

Mr. Johnson:	I haven't seen the letter from Smithson, Landon, and Levenson.
Helen:	I'm handling that one.
Mr. Johnson:	What's the problem?
Helen:	You don't need to worry about it. I've got it under control. It's a customer complaining that we didn't live up to the terms of our contract. Absurd. I've checked it out. We did.
Mr. Johnson:	I think it would be helpful if you passed matters that have an impact on our company's reputation along to me. I need to know about them when I'm in contact with the twelfth floor.
Helen:	It's really a trivial matter, but I'll give you the entire file. You'll see that we're not in trouble.

We see the secretary masterminding the strategic operations for which her boss is responsible. She is curt and exercises more control than the boss thinks advisable. When challenged, she complies grudgingly by dumping the problem back on him and calling the matter trivial.

Initiative

Asking questions of her boss and others is a high-priority activity to a 9,1-oriented secretary. She needs to feel strong in acting on her boss's behalf, and she needs to keep him out of trouble should he fail to recognize some potential consequence of an action he is about to take. All incoming mail and messages pass through her hands. She probes every item for its meaning and consequently is alert to discrepancies and contradictions.

Linn:	I haven't heard the details since you finalized the deal with Sam Brown at Acme. When will the contract start?
Mr. Walter:	We talked about some time in the next three months.

Linn:	Oh, nothing more specific than that?
Mr. Walter:	Well, it depends on the backlog at the Cherokee Plant.
Linn:	Do you know the details of the situation down there?
Mr. Walter:	No, it didn't seem to be important at the time.
Linn:	From our standpoint, don't you think it would be important to get the contract operational as soon as possible? I'll find out how things are and let you know.
Mr. Walter:	Well, that's fine. Can you have it by tomorrow?
Linn:	Oh, yes, I keep up with that situation on a regular basis.

Here we see Linn pulling information out of Mr. Walker and authorizing herself to get more information from the Cherokee Plant. For all practical purposes, she is acting as an associate manager deciding how she wants things to go and taking actions that ensure that they will proceed as she wishes. She respects the line between managing her boss by telling him what to do and managing him by operating the support system, but by her definition that line is both thin and flexible.

On the positive side, the quality of her inquiry is high, since in her thoroughness she leaves no stone unturned. In this way she gives the boss critical support. With her 9,1-orientation, she uses inquiry to shape decisions. In other words, her control over the situation is increased by inquiry and is exercised in a subtle manner under the guise of taking initiative and being helpful.

Sounding Board

By knowing as much as she does about the operations of the company from the standpoint of both open and private information, a 9,1-oriented secretary is in an excellent position when it comes to supporting her boss as a sounding board. Her data base permits her to see clearly the implications and consequences of alternative courses of action. The problem is that she may not present the data objectively, but rather in terms of her own personal evaluation.

The boss who relies on her can expect to be influenced in several ways.

First, if she is smarter and/or more thorough than her boss, she can mastermind situations so that others see him as an unusually insightful and decisive person. In effect, she is the power behind the throne, pulling the levers with only her boss being the wiser—and she may even hoodwink him. Under these conditions, one of the risks is that as she becomes stronger, the boss becomes weaker. Unless she moves up with him when he is promoted, the boss's clay feet are likely to be revealed as soon as the separation takes effect.

Second, she is likely to influence her boss by openly becoming an adviser. She may say, "Reconsider X course of action; it probably is preferable to Y," and then she presents her data to tilt the decision in favor of her preference. In casting herself in the role of both sounding board and adviser, she may also edit information that she thinks would cause the boss to move in a direction she does not want him to go in.

Norma is sitting in Mr. Howton's office, and he is reflecting on the possibility of the company's purchasing another firm.

"Acquiring that company," Mr. Howton is saying, "would represent quite a challenge to us, being in an entirely new field. However, it is larger than any we have ever taken over. That's what I'm hesitant about. I'm not so sure we've got the personnel to handle such a takeover. It would mean a costly risk. We may not be prepared for that kind of challenge."

Norma, while listening intently, can hardly contain her own evaluation of the situation. "I think it's a good takeover. We can handle it, but I'll say one thing. Someone is going to have to set the personnel manager of that organization straight. He had the gall to call the other day and ask for information I consider confidential."

"Oh? And what did you say?" asks Mr. Howton.

"I told him in no uncertain terms that the business relationship was nowhere near the point where I could give him that kind of data."

Norma taps the desk to make her point. "If we break off negotiations, he would be miles ahead of us with that information. You can't trust people like that. If we do move to make an offer on that firm, the first thing I would do would be to find a replacement for him."

Norma's 9,1 orientation shows through in this discussion. While Mr. Howton is pondering an action aloud and she is serving as a sounding board, she offers her advice: ". . . good takeover. We can handle it." This is said in a way that indicates that if he hesitates or backs off, he will be casting doubt on her judgment. Beyond that, she is using her secretarial role to cast aspersions on a manager who may become an employee. Even if it were appropriate for her to exercise such judgment, she has only skimpy evidence to support her negative attitude.

Privileged Communication

Since the 9,1-oriented secretary is aware of what is going on with her boss regarding business affairs, part of the power she wields is based on the confidences that the boss shares with her. Her loyalty lies with the organization, but that may mean that she sees herself as all-important because her boss has shared these corporate secrets with her. The boss who confides in her finds that she talks as much as—or even more than—she listens, especially when there is a third party to blame.

She is usually closemouthed, her lips as sealed as a safety deposit vault when it comes to being a source of information to anyone outside. This is her way of assuring that she is blameless for any leaks that might occur. She does not hesitate, however, to let others know that she is joint owner of her boss's corporate secrets. Even here, though, she never actually reveals the secrets; she only lets others know she has them.

Gwen and her boss, Mrs. Nall, are discussing a personnel matter.

Mrs. Nall: I haven't mentioned Joe's termination up to now because I want it kept in confidence.

Gwen: But if the termination date isn't made public for two months, how can I publish the travel schedule? You know I distribute it every two weeks. Questions will be asked if I leave him out.

Mrs. Nall: It's agreed between Joe, my boss, and me that his termination won't be announced until the first of September. I suggest you leave him out of the schedule and hope no one will ask.

A week later Neal, a colleague of Joe's, approaches Gwen.

Neal: Say, Gwen, can you find out why Joe is not on the schedule?

Gwen: *(icily)* I know why. It could be for a number of reasons, including encouraging nosy people like you to ask questions!

Gwen has no intention of letting out her secret, and she uses the occasion to be abrasive. Neal gets the message in no uncertain terms. Gwen's concern is not for Joe, for Neal, or for her boss. She has access to information few others have, and her desire is to let this fact be known because it reinforces her sense of control over others.

Interfaces

Gatekeeping

Since this secretary seeks to wield power behind the scenes, she is in her element when it comes to determining who her boss can see and when. Those who make themselves unwelcome find her distant and aloof; her allies get preferred treatment.

A phone call from a person unknown to her can yield a short, "Mr. Miller is in conference right now. I'm sorry *(click)*." If it is a business acquaintance, she may give the person the third degree before accommodating the request for an appointment or putting the call through to her boss. A common comment made regarding this secretary is, "Mr. Grant is really a nice guy—if you can get past *her!*"

Linda is busy at her desk when she notices someone in the reception area just beside her office. Realizing the receptionist is not at her desk, she goes out to greet the visitor herself.

"May I be of help?" she inquires.

"Yes, I would like to see Mr. Horn. My name is Bill Robinson."

Linda immediately stiffens. Mr. Robinson has no appointment with her boss. "Do you have an appointment?" she asks.

"No. I was in the area and thought I would drop in and see Mr. Horn if that's possible."

"I'm sorry, but you don't have an appointment," Linda replies curtly.

"Yes, I realize that; perhaps if I told you why I need to talk with—"

"I really hate to be rude, but I'm afraid that's impossible." Linda is doing a slow burn by this time. If there is one thing she detests, it's uninvited drop-ins.

About this time Mr. Horn comes into the lobby. "Bill! What a surprise! What are you doing here?"

"Well, I'm chairman of our fund-raising campaign this year and I was talking with Allen Jones earlier in Suite 211 and thought I would drop by to say hello," Bill responds.

"Well, it's good to see you. Come on in for a minute. About that golf game. . . ." Mr. Horn and Bill go into Mr. Horn's office.

Linda is dumbfounded but recovers. She quickly retreats to her office, her embarrassment overshadowed by her anger at letting herself get into such a situation. When the receptionist returns, Linda gives her a verbal warning: "Now about being away from your desk. Where have you been? . . ."

Bill probably thought it would be easier to try to see the president of the United States. With her "Who goes there?" attitude, she wasn't about to listen to any explanations as to why he happened to drop in. Linda will be remembered by Bill, but not fondly.

Perhaps the most innocent victim is the receptionist. She's the recipient of Linda's frustration, and what Linda is really saying is, "I got kicked, so I am kicking you in turn." The problem is that the receptionist may never learn the real cause of Linda's anger.

A 9,1-oriented secretary may in this manner call the shots, being "legally" right in managing her boss's time through the appointment system, yet functioning poorly by failing to consider the consequences of operating her gatekeeper system in such a rigid manner. Efficiency may reign supreme while, without realizing it, her effectiveness goes out the window.

Speaking for the Boss

This secretary is a definitive spokesperson for her boss, and this is so whether or not she has been asked to speak on his behalf. She has little time to waste, and her method of communicating is mostly one way—from her to the other person. She relays whatever information she feels is necessary and leaves it at that, no questions asked please.

She makes sure others know that she is speaking directly for the boss. This adds force in getting what she wants. Although the boss may never know what goes on, some of her reputation inevitably rubs off on him. If the boss finds out and pleads innocence, a different kind of shadow is cast over his leadership, since now others can say, "He doesn't even know what goes on in his own office." Furthermore, should the boss try to confront her with the issue directly, the secretary reacts with righteous indignation since, as she says, she has acted on his behalf.

As the link between the various persons seen throughout a day and her boss, she reveals the powerful kind of influence that a secretary is in a position to wield, holding the passkey to the boss's office. A word from her can make or break a sale, kill or seal a deal.

Jane discovers a misprint while going back over the quarterly report. She quickly dials Allen, the printer responsible for the job.

"Allen, I've found an error in the quarterly report. Have you started running the project?"

"Yes, there are about five hundred off the press now," says Allen.

"That's not all that many," Jane comes back.

"I wonder what happened . . . you approved the final copy, didn't you, Jane?"

"Of course. I did," snaps Jane. "But I can't catch everything. I suggest you correct it before the boss finds out."

"Your company will have to absorb the costs," Allen responds.

"You might consider taking it out of your own paycheck. That's a contribution that will prevent your company from losing the next print job," retorts Jane as she slams down the receiver.

Jane communicates—directly. There are no ifs, ands, or buts about it. She also makes certain she does not get caught with the mistake, and in this way she appears to be in control of the situation—at the supplier's expense. Her put-down includes cutting sarcasm. Allen indicated some willingness to confront her with the cost issue, and the sparks flew between the two. More than likely he feels defensive, frustrated, angry, and resentful—common reactions to the 9,1 orientation. Allen will probably throw his hands up and capitulate in order to retain the business, but a residue of hostility may remain that will find its target in some other way on some other day.

Speaking for Others

Because conveying messages may be critical, passing them through to the boss or withholding them is one of the actions from which this secretary derives a sense of power. As a spokesperson for others, she puts a judgment on the message or the person, depending on her own feelings and evaluations.

If she dislikes the person whose message she is passing along, she may load the message, conveying to her boss a negative image of that person in order to promote the boss's hostility toward him or her. This is done by innuendoes calculated to get the boss to see the other person as weak, untrustworthy, or uncooperative. Conversely, if she likes the person, she may load the message to convey an enhanced image of him or her.

Susan:	I just saw Joe in the hallway. He asked me to tell you he would be at the Nighthawk for lunch and would like you to join him to talk about the Acme contract. I said I would deliver the message. Then he wanted to know what you were doing this afternoon.
Mr. Hastings:	Why did he ask you that question?
Susan:	I don't know, unless he was trying to pry something out of me he shouldn't.
Mr. Hastings:	How did you answer him? Did you say you didn't know?
Susan:	Of course not, because I do know.
Mr. Hastings:	Then what did you say?
Susan:	I said I declined to answer a question he shouldn't have asked.
Mr. Hastings:	What did he say?
Susan:	Oh, he just laughed and said, "Thank you for your nonhelp," as he left.
Mr. Hastings:	Was he unhappy with you?
Susan:	No, but he learned that I'm no fool. He's not going to use me to short-circuit channels. I'm not employed to do his work for him.

In one respect, the secretary has done everything right—she passed on the message in the form in which she received it. But she did so in such a way as to cast a shadow on the person whose message she was delivering. It was hardly possible for the boss to fail to grasp her message.

The Written Word

Every letter, memo, and document must have this secretary's stamp of approval. If she composes these communications personally, they reflect her own personality and writing style. If not, she sees that they meet her specifications, even to the point of disregarding the characteristic flavor of her boss's way of communicating—that is, if her boss allows her to do so.

Betty, an administrative secretary for a computer firm, is sorting through correspondence when the intercom rings. "Yes?" responds Betty, as she turns her attention from reading a letter to listening to the caller. It's her boss, James Clark.

"Betty, I have a copy here of my memo to the committee on the new computers. I really didn't want that to go out until I put the revised figures in."

"I know, Mr. Clark," Betty replies. "But Bill in accounting wanted to have the figures on it now, so I thought it was a good idea to go ahead. I got the revised figures from your desk, put them in, and sent it out. Anyway, tomorrow is going to be a busy one for me, and I wanted to get it out of the way as soon as possible. Any problem?"

"No, I guess not," Mr. Clark responds thoughtfully. "I just thought it would be better to rework the memo and double-check the figures once more. The committee will have had time to go over the report over the weekend. Now there are probably going to be all kinds of questions thrown at me today."

"Don't worry, I edited the document and verified the numbers to my satisfaction, Mr. Clark. Any questions will have to come to *me* first, and there is no doubt that I can answer them."

"Well, okay," says Mr. Clark.

With that, Betty goes back to opening the mail, confident that she has matters (and memos) under control.

As we see here, Betty has the final say on the "written word." She knows what she is doing and what needs to be done, but in a unilateral way. Priorities for her work come first. She sees no need to check out her actions with her boss before taking them.

When Mr. Clark gives his reason for having told her not to release the memo and tells her what consequences he now expects, she also has a ready answer, letting him know she will shield him from questions.

Systems Manager

The 9,1-oriented secretary manages others with authority: "Do as you are told." Whether she manages 2 people or 50, the message is the same: "I'm in charge." Subordinates on the receiving end of this attitude may refer to her as an "old battle-ax."

Mrs. Taylor: This is your first day. I want you to get off to a good start, so I'll tell you what I want you to do, when I want it, and how I want it done.

New Receptionist: May I ask questions as we go along?

Mrs. Taylor: Not right now. I'll be clear and specific about what, where, how, and with whom.

New Receptionist: What about "why"?

Mrs. Taylor: No need. I'll tell you all you need to know. You can ask questions later.

New Receptionist: Well, I'll be—

Mrs. Taylor: Your job is to answer the phone, greet visitors, type, and so on. First, about answering the phone—I don't like the caller to have to wait. Therefore, I'll expect you to answer it within the first two rings.

New Receptionist: First two—

Mrs. Taylor: That's entirely reasonable. It means you'll have to stay close to your desk. I don't want you to say "Hello." Say "Good morning, this is XYZ Systems. May I be of help?" Remember . . . within two rings. Then. "This is XYZ Systems. May I be of help?" Is this clear?

New Receptionist: Okay, I'll try. *(Phone rings and New Receptionist answers.)* Hello, uh, I mean, this is XYZ Systems. What did you want?"

Snatching the phone from the new receptionist, Mrs. Taylor deals with the caller. Afterward, she continues the conversation.

Mrs. Taylor:	That is not what I said. Now, one more time . . .
New Receptionist:	I'm sorry . . .
Mrs. Taylor:	Look . . . pick up the phone before it has rung two times; say . . .

The new receptionist's task is structured by Mrs. Taylor, and instructions are given with a minimum of emotional support. Supervision in this situation involves complete control over the new receptionist, exercised on a "telling," one-way communication basis.

This new receptionist certainly felt unteachable and possibly that she would never make it. She was not encouraged to ask questions—quite the opposite. The big question will be, "Who runs out of patience first?"

Summary

The office climate created by a 9,1-oriented secretary is that of a command post, marshaling resources to win each new encounter. It is hurried, sometimes hectic, and rarely harmonious and warm. As a result, there is no need for "no loitering" signs; this message is communicated without words. This secretary tends to view her role as a sounding board as simply helping her boss think aloud by adding judgment, giving advice, and influencing his opinions through innuendo. Her treatment of privileged communication also reveals that her motivation is to control, master, and dominate. She lets people know she has privileged information, but she doesn't reveal it, because she sees leaking confidential information as disgraceful.

When it comes to exercising initiative, she looks under every chip to find out what is there, casting herself in the role of deputy. Yet she rarely oversteps the official line by exercising managerial responsibility overtly.

As a gatekeeper, she must always have an appropriate answer

to the questions, "Who goes there?" She admits to her boss's office only those people and messages that have her official pass. In case of doubt, she denies admission. When speaking for her boss, she expresses herself with authority, communicating directly and with finality. In communicating for others, she is influenced by her feelings toward the source, particularly when they are negative.

She retains tight control over the written word, imposing her style on it by ensuring that it meets her personal standards and specifications.

As a systems manager, she operates what she sees as an efficient business, with little regard for subordinates as people with feelings. She is saying in effect, "When someone is hurt, nothing personal is intended. This is business, and as everybody knows, business can be a jungle now and then."

A 9,1-oriented secretary places high value on doing things her own way. In terms of convictions, she is ready to stand up for her own ideas, opinions, and attitudes. She finds little reason to shy away from conflict. Winning her point of view is what counts. Her temper flares when things are not going according to her wishes. Her thoroughness is revealed by her knowledge of the details of her responsibilities, the underlying purpose being that no one catches her in error. She knows what she wants and funnels her energies into pressuring others as her way of getting it.

All of this is done in the name of production and efficiency rather than out of affection for or loyalty to her boss. She's paid to advance the interests of the company and that's what she's all about. All work and no play makes this secretary a powerful person.

4
The People-Oriented Secretary
(The 1,9 Orientation)

A 1,9-oriented secretary is the picture of geniality, a person who seeks to be friendly with everyone. She is deferential and gives particular attention to those who are left out and lonely. She tries to create a warm and friendly climate by complimenting people frequently and by reacting positively to specific requests.

She wants to be approved of and accepted so that she can feel comfortable, secure, and happy. Her way of gaining acceptance is through doing whatever is asked of her by her boss and others.

No matter how hard she may try, however, she sometimes fails to receive the warmth and approval she needs. Her greatest fear is of being rejected or disliked. When rejection does occur, it is very disturbing and increases her feelings of uncertainty and insecurity. In summary, to be accepted is what a 1,9-oriented secretary strives most to realize; being disliked and experiencing rejection are what she seeks most to avoid.

Office Climate

The 1,9-oriented secretary communicates frequently with others by means of light, chatty conversation to reassure herself that everything is okay and that people are feeling good. She keeps her eyes open for unhappiness or ill feeling so that she can help relieve any tensions that may exist.

People experience her work area as inviting. She has various plants and pictures placed around. If permissible, a radio may play softly. Her typical workday passes at a relaxed pace. Crises are softened and absorbed into the otherwise untroubled environment. Togetherness, avoidance of conflicts, harmonious feelings, and so forth, are what she strives for in her workplace.

Mr. Moody enters his office as his secretary, Leah, is arranging the flowers she has brought to work.

Mr. Moody: Good morning . . . the flowers are beautiful.

Leah: I hoped you would like them. They're so colorful. I have some for my office, too . . . did you see them?

Mr. Moody: Yes, they're lovely. . . . Has the mail arrived yet?

Leah: Yes, but I thought I would arrange these first. I hope that's okay.

Mr. Moody: Well, it creates a pleasant atmosphere around here. Thanks.

Leah busies herself for the next hour, greeting people as they arrive and catching up on "what happened to so-and-so." Only after she has assured herself that everyone is "okay" does she return to the mail.

This secretary is concerned with the physical surroundings and comfort of people who come in and out of her office. All this signals a friendly, cheerful atmosphere that is not conducive to the open expression of negative feelings. This means that important things that need to be said may go unsaid in order to avoid disturbing the warm climate.

Secretary-Boss Relationship

This secretary places high value on a warm and friendly relationship with her boss. Since she is deferential and eager to please, her natural inclination is to anticipate his wishes and desires. There will be times, of course, when differences will arise between them, in which case she will smooth over any discontent by accentuating the positive and glossing over or completely avoiding the negative.

Lana is at her desk this morning, getting ready to do the payroll for that week, when her boss, Mr. Forster, approaches. "Lana, I have been looking for a particular type of cooking utensil as a surprise for my wife. Do you have any idea where I might start? Next week is her birthday, and I thought she might like a fish poacher, since she loves to cook."

"Well, I don't know. The department stores probably have them. Shall I call them?" asks Lana.

"Oh, no, please don't worry about it. Just thought you might know. I'll take care of it later." Mr. Forster returns to his office.

But Lana does worry about it. She puts aside the payroll and takes an early lunch hour, which is spent locating the various cooking specialty shops around town. She returns to the office with several brochures and clips the particular pages she feels Mrs. Forster may find of interest. Pleased with herself, she presents them to Mr. Forster.

"Thank you, but you didn't have to do that," says Mr. Forster.

"It was no trouble; I just happened to be in the right place at the right time," replies Lana. Perhaps that wasn't *quite* the truth, but it was worth it, Lana thinks, just to see the pleased look on Mr. Forster's face.

Later the phone rings and one of the employees wants to know when payroll will be ready. Lana is quickly jolted back to reality. "It'll be ready on schedule in the morning," she replies, all the while thinking to herself, "Oh, dear. I'll have to take it home and finish it there."

Although Mr. Forster may be tempted to ask Lana to do favors for him because of her willingness to do so, he did not intend for her to neglect the payroll in order to accommodate his wishes. Lana's wish is simply to be helpful, and to experience Mr. Forster's pleasure at what she has done.

Initiative

If this secretary inquires, it is done with hesitation, trepidation, and often apology. Usually she backtracks, asks other people, or seeks any other available avenue before asking her boss. She may have to retype reports unnecessarily simply because she doesn't want to question a point. When she does have to go into her boss's office, however, it is with deference and acquiescence, plus apology for having to inquire.

The phone rings on Karen's desk. It is Ms. Nettleton, her boss. "Karen, when you have an extra minute, would you please get me a copy of the latest *Fortune*? Just put it in my hold folder."

"Sure," says Karen and hangs up the phone.

Karen surveys her desk. She has two tapes of correspondence to transcribe plus the proofing of a long report. She hurriedly puts them aside. "I'll just have to do that later," she is thinking. She dials the library downstairs to request a copy of the magazine, only to find it is not available. "Oh, no, what do I do?" Karen wonders. "I'll go to the public library."

Later that day Karen finally admits to Ms. Nettleton that she could not find a copy, nor could she check it out from the public library; she could only make copies from it.

"Oh, no problem," says Ms. Nettleton. "James had a copy. He just brought it in a few minutes ago. I only wanted to see one of our competitor's ads."

Karen's time might have been saved had she asked Ms. Nettleton for further information when she couldn't readily locate the copy. When did she need it? Would tomorrow be okay since she might have to go to the public library? As it turned out, Ms. Nettleton's wish was not a command; it was more a passing fancy. Karen, eager to please, suffered the loss of time and effort because of her lack of initiative.

Sounding Board

An important aspect of this secretary's job is being a sympathetic ear for her boss, which she likes. If he has complaints about others, she shares the concerns with him. If he bounces some ideas around, she is quick to agree whenever she senses a clear attitude on his part; but she maintains strict neutrality if she is unsure about his attitude. If he feels pressure, she gives sympathetic understanding and provides encouraging support.

Mr. Britt: Joan, I've been thinking about purchasing the plant down in Cranton. Looks like a good buy.

Joan: Oh, really? I've heard Cranton is a nice place.

Mr. Britt: There's only one problem. There seem to be a lot of union problems going on right now. I certainly don't want to buy problems; I've got too many as it is.

Joan: You certainly do. Too many problems just pave the way to misery. At least that's what my father use to say. *(pause)* I know unions can be so nasty, but let's hope that when they come to know us, they'll like us. . . . I know they will.

Mr. Britt: Well, there's always that possibility, but we have to consider that the problems are real and not easy to overcome. It may be more trouble than it's worth.

It is obvious Mr. Britt wants an audience with whom he can sound out his thinking about purchasing the Cranton plant, but Joan is not interested in the judgment side of the problem. When he brings up the union situation, she intentionally avoids the storm clouds; her primary concern is to reflect the sunny side, as she is inclined to do on most things. In doing so, this may very well act as a sedative to her boss, swinging his attention away from the negative possibility.

Privileged Communication

The 1,9-oriented secretary considers confidentiality not just a privilege but an indication of approval. As a result, she may share with her friends the fact that she knows a secret. This may cause a strain, however, because she really wants to share not only the fact that she knows a secret but the contents of the secret as well, saying at times, "Never tell anyone I told you, but. . . ." This is not done, however, to wield power, as in the case of the 9,1-oriented secretary. Rather, it is a way for her to gain the acceptance of others and avoid their rejection of her for withholding information.

Her friends know she is trustworthy in spirit, even if not true to her word. Although she feels loyalty and commitment to her boss, it is difficult for her to hold back and not reveal what she knows.

Carol is on the phone to her friend Jane, in another department.

Carol: It's ten o'clock; how about coming over for coffee?

Jane: Oh, I know what that means. . . . I'd love to, see you in a few minutes.

Carol: *(as the friend walks in)* Guess what? You're going to have a new boss.

Jane: Really? You mean Mrs. Black is leaving? I didn't have any idea. She sure has a tight lip. What's my new boss like?

Carol: I like him very much. He's being transferred back from Europe. It's a rotational assignment, and he'll be here for at least two years. Oops, I shouldn't be letting you know all of this; it's supposed to be top secret.

Jane: That's part of what a good friend is for, isn't it?

Carol: He's from Harvard . . . MBA type, thirty-five, and single, and on his way up.

Jane: Sounds most interesting.

Carol: Don't tell a soul or I'll be in trouble.

Jane: When is he coming?

Carol: Soon, but I can't tell you that. I would be breaking a secret. No one is supposed to know until the formal announcement on Tuesday.

Carol's eagerness to share information with Jane may put her in conflict with her boss over revealing the information before the formal announcement is made. She does not reveal the date of the new boss's arrival, but this is in fact a minor detail. She has gained favor from her friend by letting her in on the news in advance, and she has avoided rejection by her boss by telling her friend "not to spill the beans."

Interfaces

Gatekeeping

This secretary's primary loyalty is to her boss. However, she also wants the acceptance of other executives and administrators, and anyone else for that matter, when she deals with them on a one-to-one basis. Keeping her boss happy and maintaining good relationships with others sometimes have their strains, but they're worth it. Her reward is comments like, "You're so nice to work with; you never get upset."

"Jill," Mr. Bradley calls from the next office. "What's Roy doing this afternoon?"

Jill answers Mr. Bradley's question with an indirect comment so she doesn't have to say that Roy, her boss, is unavailable. "Well, he does have several appointments today," she says meekly. "Did you need to see him?"

"Yes, I do," responds Mr. Bradley. "I'm having a problem with this policy I just wrote. Any chance you can work me in?"

Jill swallows hard. She knows it is unlikely, yet she doesn't want to upset Mr. Bradley. "I'll see what I can do, but I can't promise because Roy is like a fly when he's busy, seeing one person for a moment here, another one there, when he's trying to help everyone out." Jill laughs nervously, making an attempt at humoring Mr. Bradley. When Roy arrives later on, she cannot fit Mr. Bradley into the appointment schedule, so she offers him coffee and donuts as her way of apologizing and preventing any possible rejection from him or ill feeling.

At first Mr. Bradley is left with the impression that there is a real possibility he can see Roy. After waiting, perhaps for a long time, he may not have such an accommodating attitude as Jill hopes he will have when he checks back and there are doughnuts instead of Roy.

Roy may hear a complaint from Mr. Bradley later on, as he will find it difficult to be nasty to Jill.

Speaking for the Boss

When it comes to good news, this secretary loves to speak for her boss and does so in a nice way. She experiences difficulty, though, when the message involves bad news, because it goes against her efforts to gain acceptance and to avoid rejection. She feels apologetic about passing a message that may make people feel criticized.

Yesterday Jan's boss, Ms. Grant, asked her to speak to the operators in the Word Processing Center about keeping the coffee room clean. Jan put it off, dreading the time when she would have to confront them.

At the ten o'clock break the next morning, Jan does not take much part in the group's conversation. Someone says, "What's the matter, Jan? You're unusually quiet today." The room seems to her to be hot and stuffy. Finally, she clears her throat and says awkwardly, "I hate to bring it up, but we need to do more about keeping the coffee room clean. Ms. Grant was quite upset yesterday when she was showing a visitor the office."

Several of the operators make offhanded comments such as, "Pay the custodian more," and "We're not paid to be maids." Jan is very uncomfortable. All she can say is, "Well, Ms. Grant would appreciate whatever we can do."

Later in the day, she notices that no one has straightened up the coffee room, so she does the tidying herself, trying hard not to be noticed.

Jan passes the criticism along but in an apologetic way. When faced with possible rejection, she smooths over the situation by backing off. Furthermore, sensing what might happen when Ms. Grant sees the coffee room, she takes care of the problem herself.

Speaking for Others

When speaking for others, this secretary is eager to convey positive information, and in her enthusiasm may even exaggerate a bit. When it comes to conveying bad news, she may literally forget her obligation to pass it on. When she remembers, she tries to cushion it as much as possible. If the boss is frustrated, she doesn't want his unhappiness to be directed at her.

The boss is asking his secretary what she heard about his recent presentation, which, in fact, was poorly received and was criticized for being inadequately supported by facts.

Mr. Jones: What have you heard?

Barbara: They seemed to admire the stand you took in presenting an unpopular position.

Mr. Jones: No criticism?

Barbara: A little, I suppose, but it was overshadowed by comments on your courage.

Mr. Jones: Are you being truthful?

Barbara: Oh, yes, Mr. Jones. People don't like bad news, but they did comment with favor on the spirit of your presentation.

Mr. Jones: Thanks. It was difficult to do and I appreciate your words of encouragement. People must realize that sometimes leaders have to make harsh decisions.

Barbara: Oh, I know.

Reacting to her boss in a favorable way is one of the positive things this secretary is motivated to do. Barbara almost totally ignores the negative comments about Mr. Jones's presentation.

She answers every question he puts to her in a way that deflects criticism and emphasizes the positive. The boss can now rationalize arbitrariness and bluntness in the name of courage.

The Written Word

This secretary yields when her boss has a clear-cut way that he wants things done, even though she may notice ways in which reports, letters, and memos could be improved. If his phrasing in a letter is awkward, she never changes it, deferring to his way of doing things rather than pointing out the awkwardness.

Mr. Reeves is concerned about his report, which Nan has transcribed accurately. On reading it over, he sees it has awkward passages that could be misconstrued, even though the data presented are factually correct.

Mr. Reeves:	I have the report you transcribed yesterday. There are several problems with it. Has it been distributed to all departments?
Nan:	*(embarrassed)* Yes, I'm afraid it has. I thought I understood everything on the tape. I'm so sorry. Do you want me to retype it? I can stay late today.
Mr. Reeves:	That won't be necessary. You can do it tomorrow. But remember to collect back all the copies from the other departments. Perhaps on long reports I should review a draft before it is typed in final form. Many times what's said looks different when it appears in print.
Nan:	Oh, I would appreciate that, Mr. Reeves. That way you'll be sure it's what you want.
Mr. Reeves:	Okay, that sounds like a good idea.
Nan:	*(getting up to leave)* Is there anything you would like to get out before I leave for the day? I would be happy to stay.
Mr. Reeves:	No, that's all for today. Good night.

Nan leaves Mr. Reeves's office, happy he hasn't been tougher on her. She'll try extra hard tomorrow to get it perfect, even work through her lunch hour if necessary.

Instead of being concerned that the report had problems, Nan was concerned with how the incident affected Mr. Reeves. She avoided his rejection and even reduced the possibility of making future mistakes by agreeing that he should be both writer and proofreader.

Systems Manager

The 1,9-oriented secretary is interested in seeing that those who work under her feel constantly encouraged and supported. She listens to their problems, making sure they have "a shoulder to cry on." She allows people to do almost anything they want to, so that the office is one happy family; at least as long as her superiors don't complain or don't seem to notice or care. Long lunches and coffee breaks are overlooked. Requests to leave early might be responded to in this way: "Sure, you've been working *so* hard today!" If her boss worries about production, she is torn between doing what the boss wants and doing what the others want. Even then she may side with her subordinates, but she does so unbeknown to her boss.

She can do all this and yet still be deferential to her superiors. This does not mean that she is manipulative. She sincerely wants to be accepted by everyone and places herself in a supportive role, trying to please one and all.

Remember the dialogue between the office manager and the new receptionist in the preceding chapter? If that office manager had had a 1,9 orientation, the conversation might have gone like this:

Office Manager: This is your first day and I want you to enjoy working here. First I'll help you go through the procedures.

New Receptionist: May I ask questions as we go along?

Office Manager: Please do, and I'll do my best to answer whatever questions you may ask.

New Receptionist: I always like to know the reason behind the procedure.

Office Manager: Sure. (*laughs*) At least I'll try to tell you why! (*continuing*) Your job is to be the receptionist. That means answering the phone, greeting visitors, typing, and so on. When answering the phone, try to get there within the first two rings. The caller always appreciates that.

New Receptionist: First two. . . .

Office Manager: Well, yes, we can try that. But if you think that's too much to expect, just let me know and I'll help you out. I'm just next door.

New Receptionist: How should I answer the phone?

Office Manager: Well, you might say, "Good morning, this is XYZ Systems. May I be of help?" I'm sure you can do it.

New Receptionist: I think I can. I'll try. (*Phone rings and New Receptionist answers.*) Hello, uh, I mean, this is XYZ Systems. What do you want?

Office Manager: (*laughs*) That's close; you've almost got it.

New Receptionist: I'm sorry. I'm sure I can. . . .

Office Manager: Oh, don't worry. You'll soon get the hang of it. Let's get some coffee. By the way, when would you like to take your lunch hour?

The office manager is warm and accepting of the new receptionist. There is no reason for negative overtones to arise. If two rings prove too few for the new receptionist, the office manager is there to help. When the new receptionist did not answer the phone properly the first time, the office manager did not push the issue but broke for coffee, possibly to relieve any tensions.

Her goal is to reduce task requirements to whatever degree is necessary to provide harmony.

Summary

The office climate of the 1,9-oriented secretary is one of warmth and comfort. Discord and hostility are not allowed to enter if they can be avoided. The physical arrangements are designed to make the surroundings pleasant, and work is done at a relaxed pace.

As a sounding board for her boss, this secretary lends a sympathetic ear, giving support and understanding. She is delighted when given confidential information because it signals acceptance. It is often difficult for her to avoid revealing it to others if withholding the information would mean criticism or rejection from her peers, but she reveals it in a "hush-hush" way. She often hesitates to exercise initiative. When compelled to, she does so with deference and apology.

As a gatekeeper, she is often torn between keeping her boss happy and maintaining good relationships with others. The same is true when speaking for her boss or speaking to her boss for others.

In helping her boss with written communications, she yields to his wishes even though this sometimes means sacrificing clarity. As a systems manager, she encourages and supports her subordinates, but little room is provided for anything but positive feedback.

Her primary motivation is to promote good relationships between people, not to find sound solutions to problems. She embraces the opinions of others rather than pushing her own. She avoids conflict, preferring to keep people together by yielding to their wishes or soothing their feelings. When tensions arise, she reacts in a warm and friendly manner. The thoroughness of her work is determined by what it is necessary to do to please others.

5
The Maternalistic Secretary

The impetus behind maternalism is the need to master, dominate, and control (9,1) coupled with the need for love and approval (1,9). These two motivations are present simultaneously but are acted upon in such a way as to control without the harshness that produces resentment or rejection, while gaining warmth, affection, and appreciation.

A recent television commercial tells the story. A middle-aged woman is seen getting out of bed, having difficulty putting her slippers on because of arthritis. She rises slowly and walks down the stairs to the kitchen to prepare breakfast for her grown children. Control here is seen in her insistence on getting their breakfast while creating a sense of obligation in them. One of them says something like, "What a wonderful mom. She insists on getting breakfast for us. She suffers but never complains. Wonderful." The camera then focuses on the mother. Through a slight demure smile, she is seen acknowledging their affection. Her refusal to let the disability prevent her from doing things for others—the personal sacrifice—must earn both the children's obligation to do her bidding when asked and their love and affection because of the suffering she endures for their sake. The term *maternalistic* is not related to any particular age. A maternal person may be 18 or 28 or 78.

A maternalistic secretary retains control in work matters, telling her boss what to do and how to do it, but in a way that never appears commanding. One of the most important elements to understand about the maternalistic secretary is how she creates a role for herself as an indispensable link between her boss and others. This way she knows what is going on in the organization. By designating herself as the "information center," she reduces direct contacts between her boss and others. She is generous, kind, and supportive when the boss and others act on her advice, recommendations, or suggestions.

Office Climate

The climate of the maternalistic secretary's office is one of "motherly" concern for the welfare of others, with encouragement to them to solicit her advice. She sees to their aid and comfort, because as they receive her thoughtful or special attention, they in turn extend her their appreciation. This concern may be manifested simply by ordering a new desk set for her boss, who, in response to his thanking her for her thoughtfulness, is told, "You're important, and your office furnishings need to reflect this." She knows what is best for "her boy" (and he can be any age too).

The office is thoughtfully arranged, with warm personal touches like family pictures or a flower arrangement on a side table and knickknacks here and there. Calmness and efficiency are projected, even to visitors.

Nita:	Won't you come in? May I be of help?
Visitor:	Oh, sorry, I thought this might be a typist place. Sorry to bother.
Nita:	Not at all. What is it?
Visitor:	Well, to tell the truth, I'm looking for a friend who works here and I got lost. Can you tell me where I can find the computer section?
Nita:	Do sit down. Who is it that you want to see?
Visitor:	Oh, yes, Mary. . . . Sorry, I don't know her last name. I met her at Sam's place last night.
Nita:	Oh, I see. . . . Perhaps you can describe her. I may know her.

Visitor:	She's about thirty, I would guess, very attractive, brown eyes, maybe 5'7", a good dancer too.
Nita:	That could be, oh, I think I know. Let me call her.
Visitor:	Oh, thanks, but I'm being a bother.

Nita phones Mary.

Mary:	(*to Nita*) Oh, goodness, send him away. I don't want to see him. I'm busy. I don't want to be seen with him. Oh, dear, everyone will know about this.
Visitor:	Is that Mary?
Nita:	She says she's tied up and will be for some time. She wanted me to explain that she's unavailable. Sorry.
Visitor:	Well, thanks for helping out. I appreciate it. (*He leaves.*)

Nita goes back to talking with Mary.

Mary:	Oh, I can't thank you enough, Nita. You saved my life.
Nita:	It was nothing. Drop by whenever you can and we will have a cup.
Mary:	Oh, I will. Thanks again.

Nita has made a friend for life by her efficiency in withholding directions and through protecting an employee from an unwanted visit, all without harrassing the visitor. You can be assured that when Mary drops by, Nita will reap the reward of approval.

Secretary-Boss Relationship

The fact is that the basic secretary-boss relationship is one in which the secretary is "the rudder that guides the ship." The maternalistic secretary is a manager without managerial rank. She exerts her thinking and inserts her judgment into problem solving and decision making, but not in an open way. What she does is influence outcomes without letting her influence be evident. In many cases, her maternalistic role may have developed after a long period of serving one boss. He has learned to depend on her in almost childlike fashion. Since she knows the business and the boss, she has developed a desire to be protective of him. This manner of caring for him in return for his appreciation is the basic style of a maternalist.

Mr. Stone:	Well, another year has rolled around. It has been our best yet, Helen, and I want to thank you for your loyalty and support.
Helen:	I appreciate that, Mr. Stone, but I haven't done any more than should be expected of anyone who wants to do a good job.
Mr. Stone:	Maybe so and maybe not, but I still don't know how we do it. I do know my decisions are better than they used to be and I feel more confident.
Helen:	That's natural . . . another year's experience. . . .
Mr. Stone:	But your help is more than just help. You have an uncanny knack for seeing below the surface. That is what is really important. You offer suggestions for me to think about. That's help. That's why I like to review my plans and proposed actions with you before I decide.
Helen:	Well, thank you. You know I enjoy the work and I appreciate your comments about my support. Not all bosses recognize what their secretaries do for them. You're very thoughtful to speak to me in this way.

Mr. Stone is being handled by a pro in the purest meaning of maternalism. She seeks no public credit for supervision of her boss. All she wants and needs is his acknowledgment. He gives the secret of his dependence away when he says, "That's why I like to review with you . . . before I decide." In effect, he has said, "I feel more confident now than a year ago, but I am now more reluctant to decide without you than I was a year ago."

Initiative

While the maternalist avoids being a busybody, inquiring is her way of keeping informed. Inquiry can be a legitimate and helpful contribution, but the maternalistic secretary often uses it to caution and to plant seeds of doubt. The control angle is related to how she used her questions, not in the questioning itself. The maternalistic secretary is warm and gracious, yet she listens, almost selectively, for what may spell trouble. This comes from her need to be protective. She can then caution and advise her boss if she sees any problems developing about which he may not be fully aware. An analogy is the way a mother seeks the details of a child's whereabouts or perhaps direct access to the child's very thoughts. The mother can then point the child in the direction she thinks most beneficial. The child may not appreciate this attention, but the mother cautions, "Mother knows best," as she gives him a hug. The maternalistic secretary does not say it in so many words, but she also sees her relationship with her boss in this controlling manner, giving an expression of approval instead of a hug.

Patricia:	I notice Grant Turner is up for nomination to the Board of Directors.
Mr. Lincoln:	Yes, we're going to discuss that at the meeting tonight.
Patricia:	I went to school with him twenty-five years ago. I've also watched his career since graduation. He's a slick character, believe me.
Mr. Lincoln:	He's done terrific things at Acme, though. He certainly has impressed the other members.

| Patricia: | Still, I wish you would check him out more thoroughly. I've heard you say time and again that he's dangerous in power plays. You wouldn't want to get involved in a power play. |
| Mr. Lincoln: | I'll certainly be careful. Funny, I felt caught up in the enthusiasm. Since you seem concerned, maybe I had better investigate his reputation a little further. |

The secretary is alert and protective about the ramifications of Turner's possible nomination: "He's dangerous in power plays. You wouldn't want to get involved in a power play. These remarks indicate that she is looking out for her boss's welfare by telling him what she thinks is best. We see, too, that her comment makes more than a little impression.

Sounding Board

The maternalist's influence on her boss is most strongly and subtly exercised when they are conversing about business matters. She is a superb sounding board because of her intense desire to know about everything that is going on, her suggestions as to what it all means, and her demonstrated evidence that she has her boss's best interests at heart.

Mr. Cook has just returned from a conference in which long-term policy issues were discussed. These are issues that may shift the direction the company takes in the future.

Mr. Cook:	Talk about intense discussions! That was one of the most heated I've ever been in.
Joann:	I'd like to know more about it.
Mr. Cook:	Good. It'll give me a chance to unwind. The president wants me to spend time on growth-through-acquisition. Everyone else wants to promote growth-from-within.

Joann:	Did you show your hand?
Mr. Cook:	Of course not. I couldn't speak first because the president always turns to his confidant, Bill, and says, "What do you think?" But I did speak last, summarizing what had been said and pointing the discussion in the direction I wanted to see us go.
Joann:	That should have influenced them. Who argued for growth-from-within?
Mr. Cook:	Well, Cecil, and he always pushes the operations manager's point of view. It expands his empire, and he prefers that to acquiring a new company that might have a reporting relationship going straight to the president rather than through him.
Joann:	It's apparent you understand him and his strategy.
Mr. Cook:	He's an empire builder, for sure.
Joann:	Who else?
Mr. Cook:	Well, Bates from finance also likes growth-from-within because of the financial control angle and accounting systems. An acquired outfit would have its own accounting system, and if it's different from ours, Bates would lose his overall grip on financial control.
Joann:	He's got a good point there. Our money controls are pretty sophisticated, and our computer studies make them a useful tool in decision making. You know how much I enjoy analyzing the summaries and telling you what they mean.

As a sounding board, Joann is listening with a sympathetic interest to Mr. Cook. By the time the conversation is completed, she will know more about each individual's stakes, the power plays involved, and which side is likely to win. We can then anticipate that she will offer her assessment of the situation and Mr. Cook will take advantage of her counseling. She relishes the self-glorification that comes from steering an important executive's future, possibly even grooming him for the top job and planning to be there with him when he arrives.

Privileged Communication

Handling confidential matters allows the maternalistic secretary to exercise control over others as they speak to gain privileged information.

Arnold:	I need some information for my planning and would like to see the boss.
Cynthia:	What is it?
Arnold:	Well, I need to know whether or not a layoff is in the works.
Cynthia:	Now, Arnold, how many times have I told you that's something we do not talk about.
Arnold:	Not even within the management committee?
Cynthia:	If I told you that, we would be talking about *it.* You know you're stepping out of line.
Arnold:	Why? I have to take the most likely situations into account.
Cynthia:	Has anyone said a layoff was likely?
Arnold:	Come on, you're not helping me very much.
Cynthia:	I'm sorry, Arnold, but I simply can't tell you. I appreciate your desire to know, but if one person knows, everyone knows.
Arnold:	Is the boss in?
Cynthia:	Yes, but he's in conference. I'm sure he would give you the same answer.
Arnold:	No help?
Cynthia:	No. Better run along now. I'm busy with finalizing next year's budget proposal. I don't have time to talk, but I think you'll approve of the

	manufacturing budget, to say nothing of salary adjustments.
Arnold:	What's in the works?
Cynthia:	*(smiles demurely)* Goodbye, Arnold.

The "bad boy" dynamic is in full sway. Arnold asked an inappropriate question and got a scolding for it. Cynthia retains her dominant position by telling him in a nice way not to ask, but she then throws out a tempting morsel to keep him coming back.

Interfaces

Gatekeeping

The maternalistic secretary loses no opportunity to garner influence, for this is her way of managing without being an appointed manager. Anyone's problem becomes her problem, and she uses her gatekeeping responsibilities to let people in without creating additional burdens for her boss. By taking a load off his shoulders, she releases him from responsibilities, and in this way she also increases his dependence.

Melinda:	*(answering the phone)* This is Mr. James's office. Melinda Canton speaking. May I be of help?
Mr. Black:	Yes, please. I need some advice. May I speak to the personnel manager?
Melinda:	I may be able to help you. What is the situation and with whom am I speaking?
Mr. Black:	My name is Joe Black, and I'm with the Bush Company. We're a consultant firm.
Melinda:	I see. What kind of consulting work do you do, Mr. Black?
Mr. Black:	Well, actually, we're a recruiting organization. We match your need for managers with a wide and rich inventory of those we know from other companies. By the way, please call me Joe.

| Melinda: | Well, I may be able to help you. If you come by my office tomorrow morning at 8:20, you can tell me in greater detail how you go about doing your recruitment and then we can see where we go from there. |
| Mr. Black: | Thank you, I look forward to seeing you. |

Melinda puts herself in the middle between the caller and her boss. Although she can help the boss by screening such inquiries, in fact, this is part of her way of establishing and maintaining her power base. She will not help if Joe contradicts her image of what she thinks is needed. If he fits, she will pick the person Joe should see, asking him to let her know what happens. If it doesn't work out, she may help some more. If it does, she will accept his appreciation and will have a friend for life.

Speaking for the Boss

The secretary again puts herself between the boss and others. In a way, she is the keeper of the keys, for only she has a full grasp of what is going on between both parties.

Marie:	*(to caller)* What can I do for you?
Caller:	I'd like to see if Mr. McCain can make a presentation at our international conference.
Marie:	That should be no problem. I presume that you will pay an honorarium. . . .
Caller:	Yes, how about something in the neighborhood of, say, $1,500? I might add that this is a very important conference. We have people coming from Mexico, several from the Far East, and many from South America, as well as the United States and Canada. It's going to be quite an international conference. It is to be held on June 1.
Marie:	Well, I'm glad you called, and I can assure you

that Mr. McCain will be most willing to participate. What about expenses? . . . Oh, fine, I'll talk
to him about this myself so I can be sure this
date gets into his schedule. I'll get back to you
with confirmation once I've worked out the details.

Later, Marie fills her boss in on the conversation she had with
the caller.

Marie: Mr. McCain, I want to tell you about a terrific
opportunity I've arranged for you. This is something I think will really give you and your work
some international visibility. Let me describe
what I have in mind. Before I go into the details,
I want you to know that if you turn this down,
I'll be upset. This is one of those activities I feel
you should definitely take part in.

Marie made the decision that Mr. McCain should participate.
She tells him she has "arranged" something special for him so
that it is next to impossible for him to refuse. This way of
directing him secures compliance before he has had the opportunity to explore the full implications of the time and effort
involved. Part of the cleverness of this strategy is the fact that
Marie inserts herself between the caller and Mr. McCain and
presents herself as the source of the opportunity. In this way she
increases Mr. McCain's dependence on her and earns his gratitude.

Speaking for Others

The maternalist sees her task as more than just getting others
together with her boss. She believes it is preferable to receive the
information and, in her role as intermediary, to edit and screen
it before she passes it along. It is not difficult for her to do this
for those at the same level as her boss. It is even easier when

those who wish to be in touch with him are from a lower level. She sets up a direct discussion between herself and the other party by talking about "the importance of the project he is working on," or by saying, "He asked not to be disturbed until four. Would you like to tell me so I can pass your information on to him when he has a free moment?" In this way she is able to intercept a large number of messages. By doing so, she learns more about what is going on than she would if she simply arranged for a direct meeting between her boss and others. She rationalizes casting herself in this intermediary role as protecting the boss from all kinds of needless interruptions.

Lucille:	*(picking up the intercom phone)* Good afternoon, Marshall.
Marshall:	Hello, Lucille.
Lucille:	What's on your mind today?
Marshall:	The boss and I have been talking about a new chemical process. He asked me to keep him posted on anything new that came to my attention. I've just learned some further details regarding the professor doing the research. I thought I would pass this along. It will only take a few minutes. Can you work me into his schedule?
Lucille:	I am sorry, Marshall, but he literally has no time. Anyway, I know something about that research and I think it's more or less a false hope. But tell me what you've learned and I'll pass it along when he takes a break. You can be assured it will get his full and undivided attention.
Marshall:	That's really great, Lucille. Here's what I've learned. . . . Okay? I appreciate your help. You'll let me know?
Lucille:	Yes, I'll let you know. I know he will appreciate your keeping him posted. Nice to talk to you.

Lucille assumes, without asking her boss, that he does not want to see Marshall himself. She strengthens her control on both her boss and Marshall by taking over the information. She now owns it and relieves her boss from another formal conference. He appreciates her bringing the information to him. Marshall is in the palm of her hand; he wants to keep on her good side because she is the primary conduit to the boss.

The Written Word

Because she is proud of her boss and jealous of his reputation, the maternalistic secretary is likely to take great pride in the compositions that leave her office. She is pleased to serve as a ghostwriter, or even as co-author or solo author. As ghostwriter, she reduces the pressure on her boss to dictate or prepare handwritten compositions by saying, "Give me the gist of what you would like to say and I'll put it in polished form." Many bosses appreciate this kind of support because it avoids time-consuming dictation. The secretary enjoys providing such support, not only because in accepting it, her boss increases his dependence on her, but also because in this way she can influence the final framing of the message. She can contribute by taking the boss's draft and rewriting it—adding, taking away, and editing as needed. She can strengthen the quality of the written word and even influence its final value as a communications product by supplementing, simplifying, clarifying, changing the emphasis to highlight the points she sees as important. Of course, she is an unacknowledged co-author in that she doesn't sign the finished product, but she does actively share in its construction.

She becomes solo author by taking some issue that has arisen and telling the boss, "I am sure I know how you would like to handle this. I'll take care of it," she says with finality. Then she writes a letter over her own signature, saying, "I discussed this matter with Mr. Jones, and he wanted me to tell you that. . . ." She has again placed herself in the position of intermediary, and it is now quite appropriate for the receiver of that letter to speak with her the next time there is a need for exchange and let her act in his behalf. We see this in the following conversation about a call from the chief executive.

Natalie: *(talking to her boss, Mr. Lee)* Larry Mays called during your trip. He asked me to tell you that a reception is being planned next week for your old friend Morris's retirement. I checked the calendar. Your schedule is clear. Then I talked to the school board and there are no conflicts. Except for some unforeseen circumstances, I indicated you would most likely be there. I'm sure you want to go. I felt he wanted you to be there to help him out. It'll mean a lot to Morris, and to you for that matter.

Mike: Thanks for putting in the protective clause and for the little advertisement regarding my role in the community. Yes, you're right. Please tell Larry I'll be there.

The secretary then writes the following note.

Dear Mr. Mays:

Mr. Lee thanks you for inviting him to the reception for Morris Turner. He has arranged his calendar in order to take part. If there are other matters I can take care of for you, please be in touch.

Sincerely,

Natalie Larson
Personal Secretary to
Michael Lee

In this example, we see that the maternalistic secretary knows how to assess the situation. She tells the boss that she is his PR person, and that it's in his best interest to go. Short of actually committing him, she has also assured Larry of her boss's likely attendance, and this is always appreciated when the invitation, as in this case, is from the chief executive's office. We also can see how efficient and responsive she appears to be in the eyes of Larry Mays. She is a person whose importance to him cannot be overestimated because of the initiative she has taken on his behalf.

Systems Manager

The maternalistic secretary manages the system for which she is responsible much as she might run her family. Each employee is treated as a daughter or a son. Unobtrusively, she studies each one in great detail, so that she learns what each one needs, wants, and resents. Having done this, she is in a position to work with all her employees to help them be more committed to the task, to help them gain new skills, and so on. By giving them clear directions, she is assured that they will avoid making mistakes. If they do make errors, she lets them know in a subtle way by reducing her emotional support and responding only when they toe the line. In turn, they express their appreciation to her, even though they may feel slightly suffocated or a little insecure.

Ms. Cantrell: I am pleased you are doing so well here, Irene.

Irene: Thanks, Ms. Cantrell. Those tips you give me from time to time come in handy.

Ms. Cantrell: Oh, any supervisor would do the same.

Irene: No, Ms. Cantrell, it's more than that. I've learned so much from you about what I should do to fit in here and make progress. Your suggestions about clothes and appearance have added to my professionalism and have helped me a great deal.

Ms. Cantrell: Well, I like to help you, Irene, because you appreciate it and you want to advance in your career. Now, there are a couple of other matters I need to go over with you. One is concerned with office procedures for how we requisition materials and equipment. The other is more important. I am thinking of requesting a word processor in next year's budget. How would you like to take a course in how to use it as a first step? Then I'm sure I can get the boss's support once he realizes that we already have developed the competence for its effective use.

Irene: Oh, how thoughtful of you, Ms. Cantrell, but others have been here longer. Shouldn't they have priority over me?

Ms. Cantrell: Don't worry, Irene. I'll arrange the same for them once we get the equipment.

Here we see Ms. Cantrell, the maternalist, taking over, telling Irene what to do and then complimenting her judgment for doing what she had been told. Ms. Cantrell takes a personal interest in all her employees, at least until they demonstrate that they don't deserve it. She enjoys helping others and being useful to them. Her pleasure comes in their appreciative acceptance of her help and their compliments on her direction. Yet her subtle control is the key to understanding the maternalistic way of supervision.

Summary

The maternalistic secretary is motivated by her need to dominate, master, and control combined with an equally deep need to gain the love, affection, and appreciation of those on whom her control is exercised.

The office climate is likely to be quiet and dignified, with people encouraged to come to her for help, advice, and suggestions of various sorts in both personal affairs and work matters. She carefully weighs her advice before giving it, with the result that the person receiving it finds it difficult not to accept with gratitude. .

When serving as a sounding board, the maternalist is likely to cross over the thin line between providing a support system and becoming a silent partner. Such crossovers, though, are not visible demonstrations of her making decisions; rather, she involves herself in the decision making by intervening in the boss's thinking so as to lead him toward the outcomes she considers important that he reach. Because she sees all the angles and implications, her boss finds that such discussions help him to think more deeply about a problem than he would normally do, and he is likely to express appreciation for such assistance. As time passes, he may discuss more and more of his problems with her. Her crossover is hidden from public view and, in significant ways, from his own view as well. Nevertheless, by intervening in her boss's problems, she creates a co-management position for herself.

In any matter that concerns her boss, she asks who said what, which issues are being supported by whom, and so forth. The boss is likely to want to give her this confidential information because her comments on what she is told increase the value of the privileged information to him. She holds privileged communications in the closest of confidence, yet she gives people just enough hints to make them come back for more.

When acting as a spokesperson either for others to the boss or for the boss to others, the maternalistic secretary places herself in an intermediary role, reducing the direct contact between the boss and others. In doing so, she gains control of vital information and in turn earns everybody's appreciation for passing along important messages.

The maternalistic secretary takes pride in helping her boss with the written word but for reasons other than might be expected. The key is that in doing so, she gains the opportunity to exercise control or influence over what is written and the manner of its expression, while fostering the boss's dependence on her.

She manages the operational system much as she might her own family, studying each person in detail to learn about his or her tensions, needs, and problems and being helpful in giving thoughtful assistance. At the same time, she gives directions in ways that help people do what she wants them to do. They in turn acknowledge their appreciation of her help.

She is decisive in her thinking and thorough in working out alternative solutions, even though these are not put forward in a way that is a direct challenge to her boss. With her conclusions clearly in mind, she can guide him in the direction she thinks it wisest to take. Her convictions are strongly held but are not expressed strongly except under special circumstances, in which she "tells" someone by extending a caution or a warning in their own best interests.

The maternalistic secretary takes conflict seriously. She prefers any option to confronting it openly because then it may get out of her control. She comes back to it later, when she has determined the best approach to take. In this way, conflict is met but not head-on; solutions are reached, but not spontaneously. By convincing others that her solution is the right one, conflict is resolved in her favor.

Because of her thoroughness and her devotion to her work, her involvement and concern make her a powerful person. However, it is not within her role to provide the solutions to problems and therefore she exercises her influence through her boss and others. The company is her life. Since she enjoys so much influence, being a secretary is very rewarding and gratifying to her.

6
The Uninvolved Secretary
(The 1,1 Orientation)

The 1,1-oriented secretary's motivation is to keep her job—although she has withdrawn emotionally and retreated mentally into indifference. This means doing enough to stay on but making little effort to contribute. She expects little and gives little in return. By being visible yet inconspicuous, she escapes being controversial, having enemies, or getting fired. She is likely to appear somewhat preoccupied, and this attitude keeps others at a distance.

The degree to which she remains tacit and uninvolved is governed by the minimum others are prepared to tolerate. By not becoming emotionally entangled with tasks or people, she avoids coming to grips with her inadequacies and inabilities and getting caught for her marginal performance. She avoids appearing bored, drifting, and listless, yet this is what she is as she goes through the rituals of completing her tasks.

Her characteristics are apparent in various ways. She is neither warm nor cold nor positive nor negative. Then how can she be described? She is bland and opaque emotionally but most likely neat and tidy in appearance. You might think she is made of wood, but you know she is alive because she breathes and moves, arrives and leaves, and in between, eats. Maintaining this combination of neutrality with physical presence is a key that prevents her from provoking undue resentment in others because of her noncommitment. Her motto is, "If I see no evil, speak no evil, hear no evil, I will be protected by not being noticed."

A 1,1-oriented secretary may not always have been passive and indifferent. She may have been actively concerned with organization activities at one time, but may have gotten "burned" somewhere along the way. Perhaps she tried to help and was rejected or was defeated in a clash of personalities and vowed that never again would she get involved with or become concerned over what happens at work.

There is a slower route into the 1,1 orientation. The secretary's involvement decreases a little each month and each year, until after several years she feels hollow. Her job has become meaningless, routine, and repetitious. She feels burned out, but she doesn't know why.

A person who has been slumping into the 1,1 orientation may be only vaguely aware of it, and if criticized, would deny it. A secretary who got stung would be well aware of it, but she rationalizes that the job is little more than exploitation: "I give and give and give without much appreciation shown in return. Companies have become so big that nothing can be done about it. They have become dehumanized and seem to be more concerned with the bottom line. I'm putting in my eight hours, so what more can people expect?" Such rationalizations are used to justify indifference, passivity, and a "Who cares?" attitude. As long as others leave her alone and pick up the slack, this secretary is content to sleepwalk through her employment.

Office Climate

The office of a 1,1-oriented secretary might be described by an outsider as dull. It might be seen by others as a kind of caretaker operation. Little takes place that is of a deliberate, calculated character, because this secretary's primary goal is to respond to circumstances as they make demands on her. She does enough to keep from being noticed for what she does not do, but not enough to stand out and be commended and then asked to do more. It is for this reason that a 1,1-oriented secretary is so difficult to recognize. Indeed, her office may give the appearance of order and a sense of direction. Its chameleonlike quality allows it to blend into the background. If it were possible to x-ray a 1,1-oriented office, the film would probably come out empty. The motto is: "Do nothing unless you are asked, and even then, do no more than the minimum." Go through the motions to whatever degree custom requires, but keep involvements strictly outside the office.

It is necessary to understand that it is possible for this secretary to maintain this approach over a long period of time. Perhaps her way of operating meshes well with that of a boss who also manages under a 1,1 orientation. Alternatively, her boss may have little need for a secretary other than to answer the phone or to make flight reservations, either because he is not very busy or because he is a do-it-yourself individual. Finally, some bosses may have inherited a 1,1-oriented secretary in an organization where no one ever gets fired, and they have simply learned to bypass her.

Here is a dialogue that might take place between a 1,1-oriented secretary and a visitor to the office.

The office is a quiet, unhurried place. A visitor enters.

Visitor:	May I speak to Mr. Jones?
Eva:	Sorry, but he is not in.
Visitor:	When do you expect him?
Eva:	I really wouldn't know.
Visitor:	Does he usually arrive around this time?
Eva:	That all depends.
Visitor:	Well, I don't want to wait if he is unlikely to come in today.
Eva:	Oh, he has nothing out of the usual planned.
Visitor:	Does he always tell you in advance whether he will come in?
Eva:	Well, not always, but sometimes.

Visitor:	What is your best guess?
Eva:	I can't say for sure.
Visitor:	Then I had better not risk waiting.
Eva:	I am sorry. You are probably better off to . . .
Visitor:	What?
Eva:	. . . make your own decision on what would be the best thing to do.

In speaking with the visitor, Eva represented the situation in an accurate manner, but in such a way as to not give information for which she might be held accountable. Of course, she did not learn who the visitor was, or the purpose of the call, nor did she offer to take a message. If her boss asks, "Who was the caller?" she says, "He didn't say." "Did he leave a message?" "No, he didn't."

Her boss's time of arrival depends on a number of variables. She does not explain to the visitor the problem of predicting the boss's arrival time. Continuing to exercise no responsibility, she tells the visitor to decide whether it is better to wait or to leave. All of this is carried out in a nonhostile manner, so she is not subject to criticism. It might be pointed out that she herself is on time so that she is not subject to criticism for tardiness. That would make her visible!

This is secretarial inertia.

Secretary-Boss Relationship

From the secretary's point of view, the relationship is one in which the boss can do no wrong because all distinctions between right and wrong have been blurred. She is employed simply to carry out his requests exactly as they are given, not to exercise her own judgment, and that is how she likes it.

Kay rings Mr. Miller on the intercom.

Kay:	You asked to be reminded about the time. You

	have just five minutes before your next appointment is scheduled.
Mr. Miller:	We are not quite through. Is my next appointment waiting?
Kay:	No, he hasn't arrived.
Mr. Miller:	Well, give me a ring when you hear from him.
Kay:	Oh, I forgot to mention it, but his secretary called to say he would be a little late.
Mr. Miller:	How late?
Kay:	A little. She didn't say beyond that.
Mr. Miller:	Let me know when he arrives.
Kay:	Okay.

Kay did precisely as requested—no more, no less. He asked her to remind him about the time and she did. Had the boss been concerned about his next appointment, he might have terminated the interview without completing the discussion. Since his next appointment had not arrived, he could use the time in a more effective way than by simply waiting idly. However, not knowing how tardy his next appointment might be, he had no idea how much time he had available. Though his secretary had carried out his instructions, she was providing a weak, unthinking support system.

Initiative

Instead of seeking information or examining implications about matters that arise in day-to-day situations, this secretary is a message taker and a message passer. She dutifully listens and even takes notes in discussions with her boss. With co-workers her motto is, "Find out enough about what is going on to keep out of trouble." With her boss and co-workers she causes no ripples, no waves, thereby calling no attention to herself.

Mr. McNeal:	I read the letter, but can you refresh me on what it said?
Kim:	Sorry, I don't seem to remember. It's in the file.

Mr. McNeal:	Don't bother, just tell me what it said.
Kim:	I've been busy and didn't take time to read it.
Mr. McNeal:	But we agreed that you never file without reviewing the correspondence.
Kim:	I know but I've been so busy . . . so much is going on. . . .
Mr. McNeal:	Is it all that demanding? I'm sure you can find time.
Kim:	We'll see. (*shrugs*)

Kim's attitude comes through as vague and indefinite. She hides by saying she doesn't seem to remember, and implies that the boss can look for the letter in the file if he wants to know what it says. She rationalizes that since she did not read it before filing, she must have been busy. Finally, she reduces the chance of any further scolding by saying, "We'll see," indicating that this may happen again if she is again "too busy."

Sounding Board

As is the case for every secretary, the 1,1-oriented secretary is faced with inevitable pressures, dissatisfactions, and an occasionally unhappy or resentful boss. She rarely if ever responds in kind, preferring instead to remain neutral and noncontroversial. She becomes very adept at reacting without presenting a personal point of view and without expressing resentment. When asked what she thinks or would do, she responds with a variety of neutral answers: "It's very complex." "I would need more information to come to grips with that one." "I haven't heard enough of that long history to have a clear opinion." "Whatever you say—you're the expert."

Mr. Green:	Here is the situation. I have told you what I understand the Systems Manager to have said. What do you think?
Ann:	Your understanding is probably accurate.

Mr. Green:	But there must be other possibilities. Give me another possible interpretation.
Ann:	Sorry, it all seems so self-evident.
Mr. Green:	Come on, you've been here twenty years; you're bound to see a number of different interpretations.
Ann:	Not really. Yours is as good as any.
Mr. Green:	But give me an alternative interpretation, no matter how far out.
Ann:	Well, I'm no mind reader; yours sounds good.

While talking with her boss, Ann really stays out of the discussion, explaining her unresponsiveness away by assuring Mr. Green that his interpretation is as good as any.

Privileged Communication

To this secretary the word *privileged* in privileged communication means that she can ignore the information. She prefers to be unaware of the facts so there will be no opportunity for anyone to criticize her for saying more than she should, for saying less than she should, or for withholding.

Mr. Smith:	We have decided how cost-of-living adjustments are to be handled this year. The announcement will be made next Thursday. The details are in the file. It tells about formula changes. You might. . . .
Sue:	So I should say nothing?
Mr. Smith:	That's too rigid, I think. Just tell subordinates whatever they ask about it, but ask them not to broadcast the information.
Sue:	Would you like to write a memo?
Mr. Smith:	No, that's not necessary.

Later the same day a subordinate of Mr. Smith's approaches Sue.

Subordinate:	What do you know about cost-of-living adjustments for the coming year?
Sue:	Nothing really, except the announcement is to be made next Thursday.
Subordinate:	How is the formula to be adjusted?
Sue:	I have the impression it is to be adjusted, but I was given no information on how much. I'm not familiar with it.
Subordinate:	The boss didn't say?
Sue:	Just the date.
Subordinate:	Okay, if that's it.
Sue:	That's it.

Sue passes on the single fact she was told. Nothing more. She has the dossier but leaves it sealed in preference to reading it and having to answer questions.

Interfaces

Gatekeeping

Screening individuals via the telephone or dealing with matters that land on her desk provides few ripples for this secretary. She is not unpleasant or annoyed, but neither is she enthusiastic, lively, or involved. She is an *occupier;* she takes up space until five o'clock. She processes telephone calls mechanically. She arranges meetings between individuals and her boss routinely.

As the person in between, she usually has excuses that serve as self-protectors. Her attitude generally is, "Why worry—you can't do much about most things anyway. If left alone, they will go away."

Mr. Miller:	This is an important customer that I am dealing with in this conference. I don't want to be interrupted for the next two hours.
Gayla:	Okay. (*The phone rings and Gayla answers it.*)

Mr. Turner:	May I speak with Mr. Miller?
Gayla:	He's in conference and asked not to be interrupted.
Mr. Turner:	I will take responsibility for the interruption.
Gayla:	Well, I don't know. He said not to interrupt him.
Mr. Turner:	It is important. I'm leaving shortly for Europe and I need to speak to him.
Gayla:	Hold on just a minute, I'll tell Mr. Miller. (*After a moment or two, Gayla comes back.*) Hello? Is this Mr. Turner? Mr. Miller will speak with you now.

Without effort on her part, the secretary takes the path of least resistance, letting the caller tell her what to do. She does this without asking who the caller is or the topic for discussion. Yet she is covered in the sense that the caller has taken the initiative and she can justify putting him through because he said, "It is important." The boss can't criticize her for irresponsibility, and she has avoided having to use her judgment.

Speaking for the Boss

This secretary knows that others, particularly the boss's subordinates, are likely to hang on the boss's every word, listening for emphasis and double meanings, implied criticisms, complaints, and so on. Her way of avoiding misunderstandings is to communicate the factual minimum and to leave inferences, judgments, and interpretations to others.

Joann:	Yes, Mr. Hickman had to leave and asked me to speak with you about the situation with the union.
Mr. Brown:	Oh, great! We've got to move on the issue of whether lubricating the machines is an operator's job or a maintenance job.
Joann:	I want to be accurate. I will read you my notes on what he said. He said we should trade out by

giving the union a five-minute extension on wash-up time in exchange for shifting the lubrication job into the operator's job description and out of the maintenance man's job description.

Mr. Brown: Did he say why?

Joann: Let's see. . . . No, it's not in my notes.

Mr. Brown: But do you have any idea why?

Joann: I had better not try to make a judgment about that.

Mr. Brown: Did he say anything that is not in your notes?

Joann: Oh, of course, he commented on this and that.

Mr. Brown: Could you be more specific?

Joann: No, I am accurate on facts, but I can't read minds.

Mr. Brown: What about a rationale for why A in exchange for B?

Joann: You can get that much better from him.

Mr. Brown: But he's not here.

Joann: I have told you what he told me. If I were to guess, it might not be correct and I might get you into trouble.

Joann has acted for her boss in what might be described as a professional manner. She has separated factual content from inferences and passed on the former, withholding the latter. If Mr. Brown criticizes her to the boss, she can always counter with, "What fact did I leave out that you told me to communicate? I referred to my notes and told him what you said."

Speaking for Others

When it comes to representing others to the boss, this secretary takes the minimum action necessary to avoid being held responsible. She knows that information from the outside is vital to her boss. If a breakdown in communication occurs, it can be traced to her inaction, but it is likely to be seen as excusable. She realizes this and takes it into account as a necessary way of staying out of trouble.

Nora Steele, the supervisor from claims, approaches Joyce at her desk and inquires, "Did you get those reports from your boss?"

Joyce looks up from her typing and shrugs. "I haven't seen them," she says and resumes typing.

Nora, apparently annoyed, gives Joyce a glare and walks away.

Later, Joyce is still at her desk. She has no intention of inquiring about the reports. She figures if Nora wants them badly enough, she can call the boss herself.

Joyce is not known as a "live wire" around the office. Everyone learns to bypass her as much as possible. She couldn't care less about whether her boss gets the message or not as long as she is covered.

The Written Word

Because her basic motivation is to be seen but not heard, the 1,1-oriented secretary prefers not to make suggestions or recommendations that might change her boss's written communication. She transcribes his dictation as given. She types items in almost the exact same form as they are presented to her. Of course, she checks the formal structure and spelling, but she does not question the content or clarity of the communication.

Frances is reading a copy of a memo she received this morning from Nina James, manager of data processing, regarding the budget meeting this Thursday. Frances considers putting the memo in her "hold" folder. Although she is responsible for the minutes to be read at this meeting, she considers them a waste of her time and hasn't typed them yet. About this time the phone rings. Mr. Young wants to know if she has typed the last meeting's minutes yet.

"Well, no," says Frances. "I'll see what I can do."

"Okay, but please send a copy to Ms. James when you get them typed." Mr. Young puts down the phone.

She looks at her notes and thinks, "They are almost legible and Ms. James's secretary should be able to read my shorthand. I'll send them over a copy right now and then I can leave. It's almost five o'clock and I have to work up the energy to face the traffic. I can always get a typed copy out tomorrow."

The next morning Mr. Young happens to meet Ms. James in the hallway. "Do the minutes agree with your recollections, Nina? I need some refreshing myself since there was such a debate that day. I haven't received my copy, but I assume you did."

"No, but I did receive Frances's notes, and my secretary just couldn't decipher the shorthand well enough to make sense out of them," responds Ms. James.

Frances has put off doing something she thinks is unnecessary and likely to be overlooked. Nonetheless, she takes sufficient action to show she is not irresponsible. In using a 1,1,-oriented approach to answer the requirement placed upon her, Frances has not solved the problem. She responded to Mr. Young's request in a slipshod way that allowed her to avoid extra work. Now others know (if they didn't before) that Frances will make some kind of response, but it will not provide what is truly needed. For Frances, producing the "written word" is an occasion for minimum compliance rather than for providing a useful tool of communication. When possible, she procrastinates until she is pressured into complying.

Systems Manager

The 1,1-oriented secretary assigns to subordinates whatever tasks must be done. With one qualification, she leaves the subordinates alone to work as they see fit, whether well or badly. The qualification is that she puts the difficult work into the hands of the most competent; the rest is handled by those whose performance is marginal. The reason is obvious. She does not want to be criticized for poor-quality work by her people. Thus even her assignment of work is in the interest of maintaining a low profile.

Rationalizing this abdication as appropriate delegation, she avoids interfering, not out of her desire to give others the opportunity to be autonomous and to learn from their own efforts, but out of her own lack of involvement.

As a supervisor, she wants to give the impression of being busy, of being at her desk, and of always being present. This way she is seen but not really noticed. However, her main reason for wanting to be seen as occupied is that subordinates are less likely to interrupt her with questions and she can coast along, continuing to do very little work.

Planned development of her subordinates is practically nonexistent in this secretary's thinking. She neither discourages nor encourages them. Generally, she feels that development should be initiated by the individual.

Cheryl is a new employee who is having an orientation with Lanell before beginning employment.

"Since you've been to the personnel department, Cheryl," Lanell begins, "I assume you know all about vacations, pay schedules, and so on. Do you have any questions about that?"

"No," replies Cheryl, "I may later, but I think I have all the information. I am a little nervous though. This is my first full-time job."

"You'll soon get over that," says Lanell. "In fact, it won't be long before you'll wish you were back in school. It gets dull pretty quickly!" She glances at her watch and continues, "I don't have anything further to tell you. When you come in on Monday, I'll put you with somebody— I don't know who yet. Almost anyone around here can help if you have questions or problems."

Taking that to mean the end of the meeting, Cheryl gets up to leave. "We'll see you on Monday," Lanell says, and turns her attention to tidying her desk.

Lanell's 1,1-oriented approach is evident in the more or less disinterested manner in which she orients Cheryl to her role as a new employee. She makes no effort to find out what Cheryl's goals are or what kind of background experience she has had. To Lanell she is just someone to fill a gap.

How Lanell supervises can be demonstrated by examining how she goes about communicating with others. In terms of giving directions, she often says, "Here's what's to be done. . . . Let me know when you're finished." Then she leaves the subordinates alone, letting them do their work as they see fit, hoping they will solve their problems by giving each other help rather than by coming to her for assistance.

Lanell is not likely to ask questions because they may uncover additional issues with which she would have to deal. She prefers to leave it to the subordinate to ask questions, on the assumption that each person is supposed to know what he or she needs to know. In thinking about a subordinate, the 1,1-oriented secretary says to herself, "If she wants the information, she'll ask for it." When asked a question, she answers it if she knows the answer and promises to find it out if she doesn't know.

When it comes to listening to subordinates' problems, a 1,1-oriented secretary is not very attentive or involved. She prefers to let subordinates talk with one another as she tunes herself out and thinks about non-work-related things. If a remark is made or a question repeated, she can always say, "I didn't get what you said." A result of this kind of attitude is that others may mistakenly consider her a thoughtful person who does not make impulsive comments or pry.

Summary

The office climate created by a 1,1-oriented secretary is characterized by dullness. Discord and hostility are not to be seen, nor are warmth and harmony. Work is not hurried, and physical arrangements tend toward the clean, uncluttered look.

The 1,1-oriented secretary is not too helpful as a sounding board because when her boss talks with her, it is more like he is talking to himself. She neither adds to nor subtracts from what he puts forward, nor does she suggest implications or offer a critique. Her approach to confidential information is based on the notion that she has a minimum "need to know." The premise is, "I can't be held responsible for something I don't know." When asked about information, she is unlikely to know much, and what she does know, she tends to keep to herself.

As a gatekeeper, she avoids either opening or closing the door under her own initiative, acting on orders and only changing to meet counter orders. As a spokesperson, she reports the facts precisely as they are given to her, sometimes simply reading from her notes. She does not see herself as a communicator for her boss.

As a systems manager, she distributes work to subordinates in a routine way, except that she assigns the harder tasks to the more competent workers.

Her primary motivation is to stay out of trouble, and that means doing enough to get by and little more. She avoids agreeing or disagreeing with the opinions of others and does not volunteer her own viewpoint. Conflicts may rage, but by not letting herself get involved, she is able to keep her cool. When tensions arise, she backs off or walks away. Her measure of thoroughness is doing enough to avoid criticism but not enough to gain compliments.

7
The Middle-of-the-Road Secretary
(The 5,5 Orientation)

The secretary in the 5,5 orientation is depicted in the middle of the Grid, where moderate concern for production is combined with moderate concern for others. We can get a sense of what the 5,5 orientation is all about by examining some well-known sayings: "Half a loaf is better than none at all." "To get along, you have to go along." "You scratch my back and I'll scratch yours." "The most important thing is to be 'in.'" Underlying each of these sayings are the guiding rules of the middle road of compromise, accommodation, and give-and-take. "The safe way is the way everyone else is doing it."

The 5,5 orientation is far more than just a passive attitude of fitting in to avoid problems. On the positive side, the 5,5-oriented secretary is motivated to belong socially. To accomplish this, she seeks her sense of direction through finding out and embracing what the majority thinks or does. Being popular means putting together a package of qualities that are sought after in the organizational marketplace, including wearing fashionable clothes, living in the right places, reading the popular books (at least the condensed versions), and pursuing other activities if they are useful for maintaining her membership in the majority group. Her desire is to make many friends, though not necessarily close ones.

She avoids being embarrassed by staying in step, such as with hair styles and fashion trends. She listens cautiously before expressing her opinion and then does so only when she is sure that it is acceptable.

Sometimes she is unsuccessful and feels unpopular and isolated from her "in" group. When this leads to criticism and loss of membership, she is likely to experience a sense of shame because she has lost her social balance and feels this is evident to others as well.

Office Climate

The climate in a 5,5-oriented secretary's office has the airy quality of lightheartedness. No one seems to be without something to say, yet little is said that is very important. One well-known aspect of the 5,5-oriented office is the informal communication system, or the grapevine, rumor mill, or scuttlebutt, and being in on this system is being "in the know." Informal communication involves a lot of talk that is not pertinent to the purpose of the organization. This includes everything from social and sports events to local political developments. The secretary's interest in informal communication is that it gives her an open window through which she can observe office members, see how they are feeling, learn what is pleasing or disturbing them, note pressure points that worry them, and so on—feel the pulse, as it were. She can then use what she learns as a basis for exaggerating or playing down announcements from higher up. She takes note of activities within the organization that have a business relevance but that are not aspects of business per se. These may involve discussions about who is coming up in the organization, who is ahead and in favor, and who has fumbled and been put on a shelf. It may involve who is having lunch with whom, overheard telephone conversations, and numerous other aspects.

Taking this secretary's efforts and interests as a whole, we see that in her organization effort she is seeking status and prestige, but not the power of the 9,1 orientation, which includes fear and intimidation. The important point is that the 5,5-oriented secretary is likely to be interested in organization politics as much as or more than her boss, because while a boss enjoys the involvement and commitment that come from direct action, a secretary may enjoy politics more vicariously as a cheerleader rather than as an official member of the management team.

Generally, she serves her boss by doing what is expected in an acceptable if not an admirable way. Sometimes she helps him by offering early warning signals about corporate affairs of which he may seem uninformed. She is able to do this because she has learned what is going on through the grapevine. The boss may find the climate she creates in the office with her friends and associates and with his colleagues quite compatible with the image of what an attractive, active, professional modern office should be.

Mary is describing to Sue her daily routine in scheduling appointments.

Sue: Are you going to have a busy day?

Mary: Oh, the usual, I guess. I have been spacing appointments so they are fifteen and sometimes thirty minutes apart. Mr. Wilson likes that. It gives him a chance to relax and we can have a discussion between appointments. He likes to tell me the main points of what's happening. Just telling me helps him get a clearer picture.

Sue: Does he ever ask you for advice?

Mary: I wouldn't say advice, but sometimes he asks me, "What do you suppose he meant by that?" I tell him, but I stick pretty close to his line of thinking. But I love to drop hints about what is going on behind the scenes. Sometimes he gets a laugh out of that. Who am I to give advice to an

executive with his kind of knowledge and experience?

Sue: Do you like working for him?

Mary: Oh, a lot. It helps me know what's happening in
the company, and I think Mr. Wilson likes to
confide in me. That helps me where other people are concerned. They're always coming to me
for information about what's going on.

We see Mary tuned in to a number of things that are taking
place in the company, some formal and related to her job
description and some informal and concerned with office and
company politics.

In terms of what is being said among people and what other
people need to know, Mary is in a go-between position. She
keeps her boss informed while making sure others farther down
in the organization know what is going on also.

Secretary-Boss Relationship

This secretary is likely to feel a "my boss and I" attitude because
she supports her boss's definition of the situation. His values
become her values. His politics are her politics. His attitudes
toward the company are hers. Within this basic orientation she
works to help him achieve his objectives. When he does so, she is
achieving hers as well.

If her boss values an office that is well appointed and conducted in a dignified manner, she thinks of many ways to show
off the office. If on the other hand he wants the office to be
spartan and businesslike, she keeps knicknacks to a minimum
and makes sure that everything is filled or disposed of as soon as
it has been dealt with. She may even dress in such a way as to
match the boss's taste and the office's visual qualities. In other
words, it is second nature for her to take whatever definitions

the boss gives and works with them, doing what she considers to be to his advantage and to hers as well.

We hear the Monday morning discussion between Mr. Wilson and Mary as he arrives.

Mary: Good morning, Mr. Wilson.

Mr. Wilson: How are you?

Mary: I'm fine. Did you have a good weekend?

Mr. Wilson: Yes, I did . . . visitors from out of town that we haven't seen for a long time . . . that sort of thing. What's on the schedule for this morning?

Mary: The usual series of conferences. I sorted your mail; it's on your desk. There's an important letter from Mrs. Jones you might want to read right away.

Mr. Wilson: What's it about?

Mary: Community Chest nominated you for this year's drive. It seems to be a great thing for you to do.

Mr. Wilson: Why do you think so? It's a lot of work—meetings, and so forth.

Mary: Oh, but you'll be called on to make speeches and to appear before groups and on television. You could become more widely known that way.

Mr. Wilson: I hadn't given it that much consideration. I'll give it some thought.

Mary: The first person you're scheduled to see is Tibbett. He called Friday to be sure that you would be in and I assured him you would. He seemed awfully nervous.

Mr. Wilson: Yes, I have some important issues to discuss with him, and without being specific I can tell you they are important to his career.

If you were to speak to Mr. Wilson about Mary, he would say, "Oh, she is a good one. She keeps things well organized and she's aware of so much that is going on. She sees the implications of what is under the surface. I enjoy our working together." On the other hand, Mary might say, "Mr. Wilson is a good person to work for. He is not demanding and appreciates the support I give by the way I organize the office. Beyond that, I try to be aware of the personal implications of business situations. This is helpful to him too."

Initiative

This secretary exercises initiative in an active but superficial way. The reason is that if she were to probe more deeply, she would risk being rebuffed for going beyond the legitimate boundaries of her role. To avoid such embarrassment, she prefers to inquire in a general way, hoping the needed information will be forthcoming. If not, she will at least have made some effort.

Betty is taking a phone call.

Betty:	Who shall I say is calling?
Caller:	Mr. Mansfield.
Betty:	May I ask the purpose of your call?
Caller:	Business.
Betty:	Yes, I understand, but can you provide a little more background so I can tell Mr. Beech of your call?
Caller:	Yes, I'm calling because a man named Sorenson, who works in your organization, suggested I call.
Betty:	I don't think I know Sorenson, but let me put you through.

Betty did her job by trying to screen the caller to see if the purpose of the call was a proper use of her boss's time. When she inquired, the caller gave her the flat response, "Business," and then added a bit of pressure without giving any real information by saying he was placing the call at the suggestion of another member of the firm. In spite of the fact that Betty does not know the person, she takes the information as sufficient reason to put him through. She has avoided the rebuff that might have come from inquiring further. Should her boss feel that he has wasted time on the call, she can say honestly that she tried to find the reason but that the caller refused to give her more background and added pressure by saying that he was calling at the suggestion of another person. If her boss says, "I didn't like his attitude," she says, "That goes for me too." If the boss says, "That was a real breakthrough," she says, "I felt I'd better put him through."

Sounding Board

The boss is likely to see his 5,5-oriented secretary as a very helpful sounding board: a person to whom he can give information, from whom he can get reactions, and on whom he can rely to keep confidential the information he makes available to her. She, meanwhile, "listens" for what is said but also for guidance as to how she should react. It all depends, of course, on which side of the issue her boss is leaning. If he is leaning toward disagreeing with some other manager on some point, she offers a thoughtful suggestion in the same direction. If agreement is deemed appropriate by the boss, she is likely to support him by agreeing. Her way of being a sounding board is to reinforce whatever direction the boss takes. He may find her to be of considerable value but for the wrong reasons. She is not helping him to think more deeply by being a good listener and asking questions. Rather than confront him honestly with what may appear to be a factual weakness or a logical error, she uses reinforcement and agreement to gain popularity with him.

Mr. Henley: I think Fred deserves a promotion.
Doris: He seems to do a good job. I know he is well liked.

Mr. Henley:	On the other hand, he botched that Lyden account earlier in the year.
Doris:	You're right, and they considered withdrawing as a client, didn't they?
Mr. Henley:	Yes, but they weren't such a hot account anyway. I think Fred came out all right.
Doris:	That's a point. Has he had any other problems with clients?
Mr. Henley:	No, not to my knowledge.
Doris:	Not to mine either.

You can almost hear the willow tree swaying. Her boss goes one way; she goes too. He bends a little; so does she. Whatever thinking the boss reveals or prejudices he expresses are reinforced through her ready agreement with him.

Privileged Communication

In handling privileged communication, the 5,5-oriented secretary respects the confidentiality involved yet reveals just enough for others to see her as "in the know." She avoids disclosing anything of a factual nature that is private. In this way, if challenged, she can always say, "I did not mention even a detail." Nonetheless, she reads what the other person wants to know, and subtly drops hints that contain bits of information that the interested third party wants. Her status is increased when her credibility is high, that is, when the secret comes out a few days or weeks later just as she implied it would. This is a positive factor in her "in"-group status. Moreover, her boss can feel that she is not a person who reveals confidences.

Lana:	Well, yes, there has been some further development on the purchase.
Larry Bates:	*(an interested subordinate of her boss)* How much?
Lana:	A little.
Larry Bates:	How little?
Lana:	Some.

Larry Bates:	Come on, you're playing games. Aren't you going to tell me?
Lana:	I would love to, but I can't. It's confidential.
Larry Bates:	Okay, I guess I'll have to wait.
Lana:	I can say I think you'll be pleased as far as your career goes.
Larry Bates:	Why do you think so?
Lana:	I guess it must be my woman's intuition.
Larry Bates:	Is that it?
Lana:	Maybe a little bit more. . . .
Larry Bates:	What?
Lana:	I think you'll be pleased financially as well.
Larry Bates:	Why?
Lana:	Now you're asking me to divulge a secret. I didn't tell you a thing, did I?
Larry Bates:	I understand . . . thanks a lot . . . not a thing.

The secretary has told "all," but she has done so while staying within the bounds of organizational protocol for privileged communications. She did not say, "Yes, this is the way it is," and she did not say, "No, it is the other way." Yet she lets Mr. Bates know in an informal way that the decision made will be to his liking. If her boss asks Bates if she let the cat out of the bag, Bates can say, "Not a word." This is a 5,5 orientation to privileged communication because it makes the secretary an "in" person, with whom confidences are shared and who respects the code of silence while making herself important to her boss's subordinates.

Interfaces

Gatekeeping

This secretary is likely to feel caught in the middle when it comes to being the coordinator between the boss and others. She wants to protect him from unjustified demands and undue interruptions. On the other hand, she wants to accommodate others who have a desire to speak with him. Gatekeeping is no problem for the standard contacts, but difficulties may arise when the situation involves an unfamiliar visitor. Then she must exercise judgment. Her worry is that she will miscalculate, and turn away someone who should be passed through or pass through someone who should be turned away.

As we have seen, her approach to inquiry is likely to be indirect, and therefore she does not gain significant benefit from responses to questions aimed at determining what to do. Under these conditions, she is likely to swing with the boss: If he says, "In case of doubt, don't," she sends the visitor away. If he says, "In case of doubt, let the person through," she lets the visitor in.

If she listens, she will find that the boss who does not want to be interrupted is likely to indicate ways of turning people away such as by saying: "He's with a client and asked not to be disturbed." Or "He's waiting for an important long-distance call." "He was planning to leave early today, and he's already gone." The boss who looks forward to being in contact with people and sees interruptions as desirable tells her, "I want an open-door policy. Anyone who wants can speak to me at any time on any subject by any means. If I am in conference, I will see them, even though it may be necessary for them to wait." By taking the boss's cue and by doing what he has implied he wants done, the secretary has in either case shifted the responsibility to the boss, with the result that she needs to exercise little or no judgment. With his guidelines in mind, she can act with great confidence and composure, because she suffers little likelihood of embarrassing herself in his eyes.

Melinda is in the conference room down the hall from her office making sure everything is in order for the visitors from abroad to tour the plant. Lisa, a co-worker, pokes her head in the door and says, "Melinda, I think the group from Tokyo is here."

"Oh, no! They weren't supposed to arrive until three o'clock." Melinda stacks the last of the papers hurriedly. "Mr. Green is in a meeting and doesn't want to be disturbed. Now what do I do?"

Thinking quickly, Melinda says, "Look, you go down and take them to the lobby. I'll wait until someone comes out to find out what kind of mood Mr. Green is in before I tell him about the guests."

In this situation, Melinda jumps at the holding-pattern notion and arranges for the visitors to gather in the lobby. Still operating by the rule, she does not interrupt her boss but waits until one of the people conferring with him steps out in order to determine how best to deal with the visitors. In this way Melinda tests the water before taking that final action step.

A more general 5,5 orientation is seen in the secretary who completely avoids the anxiety of exercising judgment; she gets the boss to tell her his rules specifically and then applies them in a cheerful and gracious manner.

Speaking for the Boss

When she acts on behalf of her boss, this secretary usually bases her reactions on what her boss might do, not necessarily on what the soundest course of action might be. If she doesn't know what her boss might do, she takes the path of what's "half right." We see that Marsha solves her dilemma in this way:

Marsha is expecting a large shipment of goods to be delivered today from the plant upstate. It has been delayed for two weeks because of material shortages, and her boss is becoming anxious.

The phone rings at Marsha's desk. It's Roy, the driver bringing in the shipment.

"Marsha, I'm at the plant, and I'll be ready to leave in about thirty minutes."

"Thirty minutes!" exclaims Marsha. "But you were supposed to be *here* thirty minutes ago. What happened?"

"Oh, the usual. The packages weren't labeled, and some of the goods hadn't even been inspected. Don't worry . . . I can make it before the three o'clock deadline." Roy goes on to explain what a terrific driver he is. "I'll even have time to stop in Albany and say hello to my brother. It'll only take a half hour."

"I don't know, Roy. You know Mr. Collins will be terribly upset if that shipment is late. What does your supervisor think?"

"He knows what a good driver I am. Besides, my brother is going to be upset if I don't stop by for at least a few minutes," Roy replies.

"Okay, I tell you what. Take fifteen minutes at your brother's home even though that is going to mean you will be pushing three o'clock." Marsha still has mixed feelings.

"No problem," says Roy. "I'll be there before you can get your vouchers typed."

We see Marsha taking the halfway approach on behalf of her boss. Being tentative and compromising, she offers Roy fifteen minutes as opposed to 30, yet by doing this risks his being late, a consequence that may cause her to suffer her boss's displeasure. Her out, however, is that she cautioned him and "forced" him to shorten his visit with his brother.

Speaking for Others

A 5,5-oriented secretary sifts the information she gives to her boss in that she says, "Here's what such-and-such says, but on the other hand, you-know-who says this." She is reluctant to approve a direction that might turn out to be wrong later on.

Lydia:	Mr. Cole, the sales representatives have indicated to me they would like to change the meeting time on Friday mornings.
Mr. Cole:	What do you mean? I thought nine o'clock was perfect for them. It allows them to get on the job before ten o'clock, yet doesn't require them to check in before nine o'clock.
Lydia:	I know, but several of them have recently decided that's too late. They would like to be back in their offices by nine-thirty in the morning.

	Apparently some of them have had some set- backs in sales lately.
Mr. Cole:	Well, what do you think, Lydia?
Lydia:	I could take a survey of how the others feel; then we could go with what most think. I did ask the other departments what they were doing, and that's how they handled it.

Here we see that Lydia's suggestion is based on finding out what the majority wants as well as what the other departments are doing. In this way she is recommending identifying a trend to define what final answer should be given to the few who wanted the change made. Since it will be based on majority thinking, she cannot be held accountable, even though some other alternative that no one has expressed, such as not having the meeting at all, might be a better solution to the problem.

The Written Word

The 5,5-oriented secretary's helpfulness is qualified by her attempt to follow the tried-and-true, "half-a-loaf" motto. In other words, she drafts a memo and initiates correspondence for her boss's signature with the following thoughts in mind: "I'll change this part but leave that; he'll buy it, I think." She's successful when she gets him to buy it whether it's right or not. It is a reluctance that says, "Test the waters first—get your boss's opinion before a position is taken."

Suzanne is going over a report Mr. Michael has dictated when she notices that a form is incorrect. The typist in the word processing center apparently did not understand the directions. Although the figures are correct, the way the columns appear is confusing when compared with previous reports.

"Hmm," Suzanne muses to herself. "If I send this back, it will mean a whole day's delay in getting it distributed. I think I'll just write a note on each copy indicating that the comparison with last year's reports can be done only if columns are transposed; then I'll send it out."

The next day Mr. Michael sees the report and is visibly upset. "Suzanne, these reports *must* be parallel in form with last year's because they are part of the company's permanent records. Please see that this doesn't happen again."

"I know that, Mr. Michael," Suzanne replies. "The problem is in the word processing center. There was no time today, but I'll get it corrected."

This is a 5,5 approach because Suzanne was willing to send out a report that is not exactly incorrect (she attaches an explanatory note) but is not according to company standards either. Mr. Michael isn't buying into her shortcut way of doing things, but she recovers by shifting the responsibility away from herself onto others.

Systems Manager

The 5,5-oriented secretary supervises by means of responsive leadership. There are many ways of moving in more or less the same direction as others, while being a little out in front as a supervisor should be. This secretary keeps within the definition of whatever everyone else is doing as the ultimate criterion for appropriateness or soundness. The result is that her behavior is conformity-centered.

Supervision under a 5,5 orientation tends to be superficial. Such a systems manager does not command or direct, and she exerts formal authority to get the job done only when necessary. Her approach is to make positive suggestions that are easily accepted in the hope that her subordinates will get the message and go along with her.

On two occasions this month Nicole has over-ordered office supplies, resulting in an obvious increase in expense for the department.

Sheila, who is the supervisor of the department, approaches her and says, "Mr. Stone is complaining about expenses again. Nicole, you really do need to be more careful about ordering supplies. You may have other things on your mind, but I would appreciate your paying closer attention to what we actually need. Feel free to order whatever you need by way of supplies, but cut down on the number of each."

"Oh, no! I'm so embarrassed at another thing wrong. I will never learn!" With that Nicole jumps up and disappears into the women's room.

"I feel sorry for her," Sheila says to herself, "but I had to stop her before it happened again." She goes back to her office and remains there the rest of the afternoon, preferring to allow time for Nicole to cool off. Tomorrow morning she can greet Nicole in a cheerful manner.

Sheila gives only surface treatment to what is evidently a work problem aggravated by a more deep-seated human problem that appears to be diverting Nicole's attention from her work. Sheila does not make an effort to find out what it is and simply assumes that Nicole's failure to focus on her duties is the cause of the problem. Even though Sheila speaks to her in a casual way, Nicole accepts the criticism as a reprimand and feels embarrassed at having been caught in error.

Summary

The 5,5-oriented secretary is motivated by her desire to be popular, to be "in," and to know what is going on. In other words her goal is to "belong" to a chosen group. She wants to be part of that group's political or social activities and to participate in its informal system. As a part of the group, she takes the status quo as given and operates within it in a pleasant manner. Her goal is to avoid taking actions that might be conspicuous or embarrassing. When conflict arises, she is certain to find out how people are thinking and to accommodate her thinking to the majority or acceptable point of view.

She creates an office climate that is bright, airy, and fresh and quite often filled with comings and goings. Many people drop by to say hello or to pass along a piece of information. Most of the conversations tend to be short, because people realize that this is a business office and it is expected to be conducted in a business-like manner. If she does have secret things to share with a confidant or an ally, she saves them for the coffee break or occasional personal telephone call.

The initiative she takes is likely to be shallow; she often fails to get to the heart of a problem.

She sees her role as a sounding board as one of providing positive reinforcement. If her boss says X, she agrees with X. If he says Y, she agrees with Y and introduces qualifications only when failure to do so would cause her to be seen as inconsistent.

As a gatekeeper, she finds out from her boss the rules or informal guidelines that he would like applied in determining who should get in or what information should be brought to his attention. As the spokesperson for her boss, she readily and confidently passes authorized information to others, and in doing so, she may shape it to make it pleasing or to reduce its negative sharpness.

She monitors the written word in order to increase the likelihood that her boss will be pleased with it, regardless of whether his written letters or other documents are in the best form. It all depends on his own grasp of how to prepare written communications.

In managing an office system, she seeks to avoid pressuring people so she does not ask for higher productivity than seems natural in the situation. She accepts the performance tempo of others, offering positive reinforcement whenever possible in order to gain popularity in the eyes of her subordinates.

She searches for workable, even though not perfect, solutions. When ideas, opinions, or attitudes different from her own appear, she initiates a middle-ground position in an accommodating way. When conflict arises, she tries to be fair but firm and to support equitable solutions. Under tension she may feel unsure as to which way to turn to avoid further pressure. She seeks to maintain a steady pace that is within an acceptable range as viewed by her boss and her subordinates. She lacks thoroughness in accomplishing tasks, often taking a shortcut just to be able to say the tasks have been completed. Knowledge of privileged information is at the heart of her feeling "in," and she cherishes knowing some of the deepest secrets. In terms of maintaining confidentiality, she is well aware of the risk of exposing her boss to criticism and suffering his criticism of her for violating a confidence.

8
The Involved Secretary
(The 9,9 Orientation)

The 9,9-oriented Grid style is in the upper right corner of the Grid figure, where a 9 of concern for the job is joined with a 9 of concern for people. It is the theory that says, "Participation, involvement, and commitment to finding and applying the best solutions are the soundest ways of integrating people into production."

This secretary commits herself to organization goals so that there is no contradiction between what the organization needs from her and what she wants to do. Her 9,9 motivation leads her to acquire the competencies required to make a positive contribution, with the result that she finds her job gratifying because what she does makes a positive difference. This is enlightened self-interest.

When an effort fails, a 9,9-oriented secretary is likely to feel disappointed and discouraged. She may be disturbed or uneasy, faced with momentary self-doubt about her ability to handle problems successfully. However, the unique thing about her is her resilience, and she quickly regains her equilibrium. She does not see short-term failure as the end of everything. When setbacks occur, her ability to put things in perspective keeps her forging onward. Her high morale is contagious.

In other Grid styles—9,1, 1,9, 5,5, 1,1, maternalism—concern for production and concern for others are seen as separate. A secretary with a 9,1 orientation might say, "I've got to have better results, and there is no way to get them without putting pressure on my boss." A 1,9-oriented secretary says, "I don't worry about setting any records as long as my boss is happy." A maternalist says, "When people show their loyalty by doing what is asked of them, they deserve to be treated well." A 5,5-oriented secretary sees her work as a balancing act; she does an acceptable amount for her boss and keeps complaints from him to a minimum. A 1,1-oriented secretary prefers to hide problems rather than deal with them. Secretaries with any of these Grid styles see things as either-or or neither. They set up false assumptions and then act on them.

On the other hand, a belief that high concern for results is best achieved through a high concern for people leads to this: The two high concerns become unified into a new, distinctive way of solving problems. The resulting interdependence between secretary and boss causes these two to look at problems in a way that produces synergy: Together they come up with solutions that are sounder than either would have reached without the help of the other.

Office Climate

The working environment of a 9,9-oriented secretary is characterized by openness and by support for and encouragement of achievement. Other people find this secretary's office a place where problems can be discussed and thrashed out without fear that they are walking onto a win-lose battlefield. Visitors find her cordial and courteous, a good listener. She involves herself— whether she is representing her boss or supervising others—in each situation and in so doing encourages and obtains the active participation of others. The boss maximizes her contribution to his effectiveness by seeing her and the support system as a resource for accomplishing corporate objectives.

Christine: *(talking to subordinates Sue and Glenda)* I received a call yesterday from Mr. Lemons.

Sue:	What'd he say?
Christine:	He wants to develop a complete training program for approximately two hundred technicians.
Glenda:	Wow, that's fantastic!
Christine:	Yes, except that he wants the complete course typed right away. It contains many specific technical training modules. We have three people in word processing who would be good on that because they know the technical jargon. The only problem is that they're all tied up on other projects. I don't know how in the world they would have time to do what he's asking.
Sue:	Maybe you should talk with him about what specific target date he has. A lot of times people will say they want a job immediately, but when you get right down to it, it's not as much of a rush as it sounds. Maybe we could break in someone else on the job.
Christine:	Well, we want to make sure; it sounded like a rush job to me, so I guess I need to talk to him again.
Glenda:	When you do meet with him, a couple of word processing people could go with you. They're in a good position to understand what is needed and how it can be done.
Christine:	I see no problem with that. But will we be getting too many people into the act?
Sue:	At least take June. I know she's tied up on her project, but she's got the best knowledge for evaluating that particular technical area. You can count on her opinion.
Christine:	I'll speak to her about it. Then I'll call Mr. Lemons and ask him when we can meet.

Christine realizes that the first definition of what Mr. Lemons needs may not be the ultimate one and that experts are available who may be able to see additional or alternative ways of dealing with the problem. This 9,9-oriented secretary recognizes an opportunity to organize and to provide a service in a technically sound way. She is also open to Sue's and Glenda's suggestions and advice in solving the problem.

We see the climate as one in which all are prepared to contribute their own thinking and where nothing is taken for granted. They probe to find the real facts and are open to suggestions so that the best way for dealing with the situation can be found. The atmosphere is one in which problem solving is central, yet it is undertaken in such a way that people are used to and willing to participate—to their full potential.

Secretary-Boss Relationship

A 9,9-oriented secretary understands the difference between providing a strong support system and becoming excessively involved in problem solving and decision making. The two—problem solving and decision making—are interwoven, but each is nevertheless a distinct process. While the secretary is party to many of the issues involved and may have significant input to offer, her greatest contribution is her commitment to the course of action decided upon because she has participated in the decision-making process.

Mr. Fogle is preparing for a meeting with the principals in the Australian account.

Mr. Fogle: Margie, I need a reconstruction of the whole problem surrounding the contract terms for the Australian project. Would you please assemble all telephone résumés, memoranda, and informal notes that I have put into the Australia file.

	As you review them, note any outstanding issues that need further research.
Margie:	Okay, but this may take some time. When do you need it?
Mr. Fogle:	By Thursday. Can we review it some time Wednesday so I'm prepared for the Thursday meeting?
Margie:	That's fine.
Mr. Fogle:	When you get a chronology of the thing set up, I'd like a double-spaced draft so I can make notes on it.
Margie:	Okay. Last time we found that some of those résumés didn't contain all the pertinent data, and there weren't enough clues to fill in the whole story.
Mr. Fogle:	That's true . . . ask me anything you want. I may be able to fill in gaps or possibly suggest where additional information can be found.
Margie:	I've never really known all the details about the key problems with Australia myself. This should be interesting.

Here we see 9,9-oriented secretary-boss interdependence. The relationship is open, and each is involved in thinking through how to meet Mr. Fogle's need for information in the best and fullest way. The secretary's support is in preparing the documented summary she has been asked to make, but the boss realizes that he has personal knowledge that may be essential for her to have if she is to give him the best possible product. Therefore, he makes himself available for questioning as needed so that she can discharge her part of the responsibility.

Initiative

A secretary has to exercise initiative in delving into the causes of problems and finding solutions to them. She must also exercise initiative to keep informed about facts and figures. A 9,9-oriented secretary expects to inquire to find out underlying details. She feels a need to inquire in order to gather necessary data or to assess the facts involved in order to have the whole picture. This helps her perform more effectively.

Janice: Before you call Mr. Jenkins about those bid figures, I would like to look them over. At first glance they don't check out compared with last month's figures. Do they seem okay to you?

Mr. Cross: Oh, they should be okay. The association is usually very accurate in their weekly figures.

Janice: Still, I've seen them too many times and this week's figures appear off. It won't take me fifteen minutes to check them out.

Mr. Cross: Good idea. If you think they're not accurate, they should be checked out.

While her boss was prepared to take the third party's word at face value, Janice's first glance lit a warning signal on the accuracy of the figures and she pressed for a double check. Whether the figures were incorrect or not, she was conscientious about the importance of accuracy and took the responsibility for ensuring it. The matter of inquiry is very important in providing a strong support system.

Sounding Board

This secretary reacts to the boss's opinions, generalizations, and information sharing on the premise that "two heads are better than one." Knowing that the boss is on a higher level in the organization does not prevent her from openly expressing her thoughts and feelings about issues being discussed. She acts on the assumption that what she says will be considered, weighed, and reacted to in a forthright and candid manner.

Mr. Grant is discussing with Janet the site of next year's annual national meeting of sales representatives.

"There have been numerous complaints about the hotel and even about some of the speakers we had," Mr. Grant says.

"Yes, I recall," responds Janet. "Some of the sales representatives' wives called me and voiced their concerns. Almost all of them expressed disappointment with the hotel."

"It's such a well-known place that it was a surprise that their facilities and service were lacking. But those things happen. Now we'll just have to make sure we don't make the same mistake twice." Mr. Grant continues to thumb through the hotel brochure as he is talking.

"You'll see in the packet sent by the Chamber of Commerce," Janet points out, "that there are three possible hotels near the conference center where we might meet next year. Maybe Joe Miles could check them out next month. He'll be there for a regional meeting anyway, and he can check them out to make sure the service they commit themselves to provide meets our needs."

"I was thinking I'd better check them out myself some weekend, but that's a better idea. I'll give Joe a call right now. Thanks, Janet. By the way, can I ask him to get together with you to review the specific points we want to know about?"

"Oh, sure. I've got a whole checklist in my mind. I'll type it up so Joe and I can have a good detailed review when he comes back at the end of next month. That should give us plenty of time to make all the arrangements for the sales meeting."

Creative give-and-take is evident in the discussion of Mr. Grant's problem. And we see that the approach to the problem is far different from the one he had in mind initially. The benefits of this kind of a sounding-board relationship are that new avenues are explored, information potentially available is brought into use, and implications that might not have been obvious are considered. These are the kinds of contributions possible when the secretary-boss relationship permits both to interact on the basis of shared participation, involvement, and commitment.

Privileged Communication

Whatever confidential information the 9,9-oriented secretary possesses is kept just that way—confidential. She sees this aspect of her position as essential to the smooth interrelationships between her, her boss, and other members of the organization. Therefore, she keeps confidential information to herself, realizing that the more she knows, the more she can contribute, but acknowledging that there are sound reasons for others to not have access to privileged information through her. Her boss is confident that corporate secrets passed to her will go no further. She is unassuming about having the ear of the boss. When company members want access to confidential information, they know they will have to seek it elsewhere.

Mr. Cruise is discussing an employee transfer with his secretary, Anne.

Mr. Cruise:	Bruce is terribly unhappy in his department. I am afraid there is a personality clash with Bill. At any rate, it is affecting his work. He told me he is thinking seriously of leaving.
Anne:	I hope not. Are there others with whom he doesn't get along?
Mr. Cruise:	Joe, and I'm not surprised. He's very difficult at times also.
Anne:	What might happen if you and Bruce met first with Bill and then with Joe to talk it out? Would it produce an explosion?
Mr. Cruise:	Well, I think it might be safer to talk to each of them individually to try to get all the facts together and then diagnose what the real problem is. Would you make separate appointments with all three of them as soon as possible?

Later Joe calls Anne on the intercom.

Joe:	Do you know what Mr. Cruise wants to talk to me about?
Anne:	He asked me to set up an appointment. That's about all there is to say at this point, Joe.
Joe:	Bruce is always crabbing about something. Now what am I going to be accused of?
Anne:	That sounds a little self-incriminating to me, Joe. But, seriously, I am not the one to ask. The thing to do is to bring it up with Mr. Cruise.
Joe:	You bet I will. I'm not going to be intimidated.

This answer by Anne was objective and to the point. The purpose of Mr. Cruise's discussions with Joe and Bill is to get to the heart of the problem, not to get a prepared defense as might have happened had Joe been forewarned. It was not Anne's place to give details to Joe and she indicated this. Had Anne revealed the confidence, she would have ultimately become a part of the problem.

Interfaces

Gatekeeping

This secretary realizes the importance of scheduling an appointment with her boss or of handling a call in a sound way because the person seeking a contact has issues that are significant to him or her and potentially to her boss. Equally important, her boss's concerns and activities may or may not fit in with the caller's business. Her motivation is to fit the concerns of those seeking to contact her boss with his concerns and priorities. Sometimes she cannot reconcile these two sets of needs and then her boss is called upon. Her position at this point is to maintain objectivity by not taking sides and by remaining aware of her in-between position.

In the following example we see some of the inevitable conflicting pressures:

In her boss's absence Mildred helps Tom solve his dilemma.

Tom: That's the story. I see it as something of an emergency. Production drops 20 percent when one line is down.

Mildred: What are you thinking about doing?

Tom: Well, if the boss will approve it, $5,000 will buy the equipment we need to get the line back on stream. Can you authorize that?

Mildred: No, I can't.

Tom: Can you put me in touch with the boss?

Mildred: I'm sorry, I can't do that either. He's on a white water boat trip down the Colorado.

Tom: So what do I do, sit on my thumbs while production suffers?

Mildred: No, not exactly. I think the equipment you need lies unused and in good shape at the warehouse across town. Did you know that?

Tom: Well, yes, you're right . . . now that you mention it. I'd forgotten all about it. Who can authorize me to move it?

Mildred: I can arrange it in five minutes. It's controlled by the security people. If you tell me you want it, then I will use that as authorization to get it released.

Tom: Okay, get in touch with the security people and I'll have someone there to pick it up in about two hours. Thanks for thinking about my problem. You're a lifesaver.

Mildred takes responsibility for contributing to the solution of the problem in her boss's absence but does so within the limits of her authority. Because she has a total feel for the facts and figures, she can act as a representative of her boss by thinking about the problem as he might have done had he been present.

Speaking for the boss

The 9,9-oriented secretary is objective and accurate when speaking on her boss's behalf. Confident of her facts, she does not hesitate to offer suggestions or alternatives to the other party. She realizes that many times she may not know the answers to all the questions submitted to her and therefore she uses the resources of others to find necessary information.

Frances, the secretary to Mr. Gilchrist, is speaking on the telephone to the department manager, Mr. Pollin.

Frances:	Hello, Mr. Pollin. Mr. Gilchrist just phoned from New York and gave me a message for you.
Mr. Pollin:	How is the deal coming? Anything signed yet?
Frances:	No, but Mr. Gilchrist said that progress is being made.
Mr. Pollin:	Have they bought the delivery date?
Frances:	I'm not familiar with the details of the meetings, but Mr. Gilchrist expressed some concern about overloading our capacity. He asked me to set up a conference with you the day after tomorrow in the morning. Do you think that is possible?
Mr. Pollin:	Sure, that's okay by me. I bet he'll put the squeeze on me for an earlier delivery date.
Frances:	I'll be glad to call and give him any additional information you have, or I could arrange for you to call him.
Mr. Pollin:	Okay, let's do everything we can to get the business. I can speed up the delivery date if that's what it takes.
Frances:	Do you want me to tell him that?
Mr. Pollin:	Yes, it will encourage him to know I'm on the team for getting this contract. Yes, if you will, tell him.
Frances:	Thank you.

She passes along her boss's request for an appointment in a straightforward way. Sensing the need to close a communication loop, she offers her support to ensure that needed actions are taken, at the same time refraining from speculating on the deal or adding to rumors. In doing this, some of Mr. Pollin's resistance about the delivery date begins to crumble, and she is able to tell her boss of his more flexible attitude about the delivery date.

The example gives an indication of how a secretary can make contributions. She is being more than a reliable message passer, by having in mind what her boss needs to know in order to be effective himself. This is an example of how, through having a wide perspective, a secretary can help others see themselves and their own contributions in a broader context.

Speaking for Others

When it comes to representing others, this secretary takes informal inquiries and puts them together in a pattern, gets her facts straight, and presents them.

Brigitte is representing the concerns of several people to her boss, Mr. Cobb.

Brigitte: Something is worrying me.
Mr. Cobb: Yes?
Brigitte: Several people have called with questions about the new benefits package. It appears it is just not understood.
Mr. Cobb: But I thought my memo was self-explanatory.
Brigitte: I know, but the questions keep cropping up, particularly about the employee contribution to the benefits package and how it comes into effect. There also seem to be other areas of confusion.
Mr. Cobb: Maybe it's just a matter of people getting used to it.

Brigitte:	Possibly, but I don't think so. It must be too complicated for easy interpretation.
Mr. Cobb:	So you think it's written like a rules and regulations form?
Brigitte:	Yes, I do.
Mr. Cobb:	Okay. I will bring it up in this morning's meeting and try to find out what the real problem is. It's absurd to develop an excellent benefits package and then have people fail to understand it.

In speaking for others, Brigitte takes the opportunity to conclude from the queries she has received that there is a problem with the boss's memo. Convinced that she is reading the situation accurately, the boss agrees to review the problem. As a result, it is likely that discussions will take place to rectify any misunderstandings about the package. At least two consequences are likely because Brigitte confronted the boss with an issue she felt deserved further attention. Her boss's responsiveness to legitimate concerns will be shown. And there will be a chance to clear up the annoying confusions. Brigitte sees her job as one of anticipating what the boss needs to be told, as well as accurately representing the opinions of others.

The Written Word

The goal of the 9,9-oriented secretary is for correspondence to meet professional standards, to be correct and coherent. She may accomplish this by clarifying messages that her boss has written that she knows do not convey his meaning, or she may add information that he had not thought to include. When she is uncertain as to errors of structure or content, she brings them to the attention of her boss or others to double-check for the correct form or meaning.

Donna is reading through the manuscript she has typed for her boss. She notices several phrases that are redundant and pencils in question

112 The Secretary Grid

marks in the margin. She places the manuscript on Mr. Green's desk for his review.

Later Mr. Green comes into her office and says, "Donna, I'm not sure what you are questioning here."

"It comes across to me as repetitive," Donna replies. "On page 13 the explanation is very much the same as on page 9."

"Well, I don't see any reason to change it at this point. We'll let the publisher's editor worry about it. Anyway, most people probably won't notice. You're just too particular." Mr. Green chuckles as he flips through the pages.

"That may be true, Mr. Green, but the editor may not pick it up because she's not as familiar with the content as we are." Donna also explains that reader complaints are always directed to the author, not the publisher.

"You're right. Please do fix it," says Mr. Green after thinking for a moment. "Are there others too?"

"Yes, there are. I'll fix them all at once and give you a final look."

Here we see Donna challenging Mr. Green's lower standards of performance. Her concern is that the material be well written. The result is that the completed document will be of higher quality than otherwise would have been the case. Donna does more than apply a mechanical standard for correctness of detail; by taking the reader's point of view, she ensures that the message comes through.

Systems Manager

In order to get the soundest actions to be taken, the 9,9-oriented secretary strives for commitment in her subordinates. One way that she does this is through effective communication. Authentic communication means she doesn't alter the message just to make it more acceptable. She presents problems honestly, objectively, and realistically. She describes a given problem in terms of what the current difficulties are, what she sees to be the causes, and what she sees to be the likely consequences. She may also indicate possible solutions if she has clear-cut ideas as to what a good solution might entail.

Thus, she involves subordinates in determining why things need improvement and gains their commitment to positive action.

Today Ellen receives word from the publisher that in order for her boss's book on chemistry to be considered for the spring selections they must receive the final typed version in two weeks. The problem this presents is that the two typists Ellen supervises are experiencing a typing backlog. She estimates it will take at least four days to catch up.

Ellen calls the typists, Joann and Gail, into her office to discuss the situation. "I don't have four hands!" is Gail's first reaction. "You'll just have to tell them they have to accept the delay in receiving the book," Joann says.

"Well, wait a minute," cautions Ellen. "Let's look at how we can solve it. Don't we have some alternatives?"

"Come to think of it," Gail replies, "we do use the temporary service occasionally. Could they help with the manuscript?"

"Well, they could pick up some of the routine backlog. They don't do manuscript typing very well, and some of those chemical equations are difficult. But since they have the same type of equipment we have, there would be no problem at all giving them some of our other work," Ellen responds.

"I'll be glad to pick up or delivery copy on my way to work. It's right on my way," says Joann. "And we could schedule certain times to proofread their work."

"That's a good idea," responds Ellen. "But let me check with the typing service first to see if they can work us in."

Joann interjects, "I will also ask around the other departments and see if there is a typist who might be available to help us out for a day or two."

Ellen's managerial approach is to involve those who can help in solving problems. Her request for alternative thinking resulted in creative solutions from Gail and Joann. What could have been a failure was turned into a success through participation and involvement. Ellen uses the same standards for problem solving with those who report to her as she does with her boss. This reliance on finding solutions to problems with and through participation is an important key to the 9,9-oriented approach.

Summary

The 9,9-oriented secretary realizes that the soundest way to perform and enjoy her work is to make a contribution that is positive and constructive. This is reflected in the way she helps the organization by assisting her boss to discharge his responsibilities in the fullest possible way. She avoids acting out of selfish interest.

The office of a 9,9-oriented secretary tends to be open and easily entered by anyone who has business to conduct. This openness is accompanied by a friendliness that makes her office an enjoyable place. On the other hand, it is not the kind of openness and friendliness that invites chitchat and gossip.

Where initiative is concerned, she does not hesitate to exercise it; she takes little or nothing for granted. She ensures that her boss is provided with as much relevant information as is available, points out data that are unavailable or missing, and when possible, develops those data as a way of exercising personal initiative.

She recognizes the importance of actively listening to her boss to understand his thinking. She refrains from offering advice, but she challenges unjustified assumptions, and conclusions based on insufficient data, and offers alternative explanations for different conclusions. Her primary purpose is to help her boss come to sound conclusions by aiding him in clear thinking and analysis. This is true teamwork.

As a gatekeeper, she ensures to the best of her ability that people who need appointments get appointments and that information her boss needs comes to his attention. She expresses herself with assurance when speaking for her boss, communicating his thoughts clearly and directly. When it comes to the written word, she ensures that what leaves the office is in proper form with regard to structure and spelling and that the message conveyed is accurate and understandable. When managing an operational system, she seeks to gain the commitment of her subordinates to standards of excellence for productivity, quality, punctuality, and so forth, and to involve them in finding solutions to problems that affect them.

She places high value on sound decisions and is creative in reaching these decisions. She is forthright in letting others know where she stands but is prepared to shift when faced with better thinking, additional data, or other evidence that contradicts convictions that she held previously.

Her approach to conflict is to focus on it, confront it, and resolve it. In this way, misunderstandings and disagreements are dealt with as they arise and little opportunity is left for them to smolder.

She does not lose her temper easily, but when unnecessary barriers arise, she becomes impatient. Her thoroughness is seen in her inquiry into the meaning of things as well as in her alertness to subtle discrepancies and contradictions. She concentrates her energy on the situation in an enthusiastic manner, and this draws involvement and commitment from others.

9
The 9,9 Approach to Managing Office Routines

There are common threads that run through good office routines. It is appropriate to examine these common threads of thoroughness, planning, time management, and expectations as viewed in a 9,9-oriented way. This will help you double-check your own thinking as you complete your daily tasks.

1. *Thoroughness.* This means you have the inclusive, factual information and details in your mind to deal with each situation in a well-organized manner.
2. *Planning.* You plan ahead in order to respond to people and situations in a thoughtful way.
3. *Time management.* You arrange activities in a meaningful sequence and allocate sufficient time to deal with each one so as not to fall behind or become buried in paperwork.
4. *Expectations.* You consider and, in an effective way, anticipate what others need from you by way of support in order to improve the total operation.

You will see these 9,9 kinds of behavior in the following examples of how a secretary can organize her work. These particular activities, when done in a thoughtful way, can help a new secretary make a very effective entry into her job.* They can also serve as a self-appraisal checklist for an experienced secretary.

*L. B. Belker, *The Successful Secretary* (New York: AMACOM, 1981).

9,9-Oriented Behavior

Being on Time

If working hours are from nine to five, you are well advised to keep on this schedule, at least until any change has been discussed with your boss, such as an organization shift to use flexitime or a need for a different schedule in order for you to better carry out the work of your office.

It is always a good idea to be punctual. This is so even if it doesn't seem to matter to the boss and even if other secretaries keep different schedules. It is as easy to arrive on time as it is to always be late. It is a matter of anticipation and organization on your part, and your punctuality leads others to feel that they can depend on you.

Note that this may cause you to appear somewhat rigid in the eyes of other secretaries who may be more lax, but it is better to respect the established schedule than to follow the example of others. This also applies to lunch time and other breaks built into the daily routine.

Managing the Office

Opening the Mail

It is common for secretaries to open the mail. The subtlety here is in anticipating how the boss prefers mail to be organized prior to his receiving it. Sorting and organizing items as they are opened as well as being familiar with their contents are one way of increasing effectiveness by better time management for you and your boss.

A standard procedure is to sort important business mail from junk mail. Even though this distinction is not always easy to make, you can automatically separate mail into two different groups: one of higher and one of lower priority. As a matter of fact, in the beginning you might want to separate correspondence that you may have questions about from correspondence that is more straightforward. Then you can inquire as to the best handling of the correspondence that is in doubt.

The next step is to provide the boss with relevant backup information from the files with respect to each letter. A good rule of thumb to follow is this: If the letter refers to prior agreements, commitments, or correspondence, it may be worthwhile to present the correspondence clipped to the pertinent file. If the boss does not want the file, he will let that be known and little harm will have been done; if he does, you have helped him by having it there already.

If the letter refers to a prior agreement in another file, policy, or contract, both the direct file and the supplementary file may need to be correlated. This may be more than is needed; therefore, it may be better to ask the boss first. The important point here is not to double-think the boss before you have experience in working with him, but rather to be alert to alternatives and possibilities, which will make it easier for him to help you become acquainted with your responsibilities. Developing solid expectations can do much to strengthen the support system you provide.

There is also the mail marked "personal and confidential." Whatever the reason for the confidentiality, you can respect it by giving it to the boss unopened. He will let you know if that is the way it should be handled or if it should be opened along with the rest.

Touching Base with the Boss

Your boss may schedule brief planning meetings with you the first thing in the morning to review what is expected to happen and to wrap up details left incomplete the previous day. This can include going over the list of people to be contacted for any meetings to be held, reading through agendas, mentioning phone calls to be placed, and so on. If there is an appointment diary, it may be worthwhile to determine who is expected and what files may be needed. Giving the needed files to the boss at the beginning of the day or prior to meetings is much more time efficient than waiting for him to say, "Please get me the Jones file." This kind of anticipation and planning can contribute greatly to being on top of details rather than being buried in them.

Placing Calls and Answering the Phone

When the boss wants to speak to someone on the phone, he may ask you to place the call. In most instances there are no difficulties, except that the boss may assume you know more about the person than you do. Since it may be burdensome to the boss to supply the details of area codes and telephone numbers, it is important to master them as rapidly as possible.

From the beginning it may be worthwhile to log telephone calls made, so that frequently called numbers can be quickly identified and placed into a system that can be consulted when the boss says, "Please get Jones on the phone."

There are many ways of making a request of another secretary when placing a call for your boss that convey your consideration of her and aid in completing the transaction. One way is to say, "Mr. Smith [your boss] would like to speak with Mr. Shelton. Is it possible for him to take the call?" If she says yes, the problem is solved. If she says no, you may ask, "Will he be available later on?" In all probability Mr. Shelton's secretary will tell you why he is unavailable. You can then decide whether to ask her to have Mr. Shelton call your boss, or whether it might be better for your boss to call back. If you leave a message for Mr. Shelton to return the call, his secretary may or may not forward the request to him; if she does, he may not return the call. Therefore, if it is a matter of importance to your boss, it may be better to call back. All of these are judgment decisions on your part.

An informative way of answering your phone is, "This is Mr. Smith's office. May I help you?" If your boss is unavailable and you are dealing with the caller's secretary, as above, you may say,

"He should be able to return the call later today. May I leave him a message?" You may also ask, "Is there a message you would like me to give him before he returns your call?" It is a good idea to tell the caller's secretary the circumstances, if appropriate, and when you expect he will be able to return the call. Little harm is done by providing this background information, and much is gained because the caller has a good indication as to when to expect a return call. It is hard to overestimate the significance of fulfilling the expectations of a caller that a message will reach your boss and that the caller will get a response. As a 9,9-oriented intermediary, you can ensure that these vital links between people take place.

Keeping an Appointments Schedule

One of the conspicuous features of organization life is that people make appointments to see one another, either on a one-on-one basis or when several convene for a meeting. Some are impromptu huddles, but many are planned in advance.

Scheduling your boss's appointments is done best by keeping an hour-by-hour calendar appointment book that provides adequate space for jotting down the name of the visitor and sometimes the purpose of the visit. It may be desirable to have a year's schedule, as some appointments are made well in advance. This is also true for managers who make field trips, who attend the meetings of professional societies, or who have formal commitments (meetings, presentations, etc.) in which they are scheduled to take part.

You are in an excellent position to keep this type of appointment schedule, and it is important for you to do so because this is vital information in your planning. For example, in a telephone call someone may say, "I will be out of town until next Wednesday and would like to see Jim that day. What does his appointment schedule look like?" You can immediately refer to it and answer back, "I am sorry, he is scheduled throughout that day, but he does have time on Thursday. Would that be satisfactory?"

It is obvious, then, that managing the boss's schedule permits a smooth flow of activities and makes an important contribution to his time management. There are few routines that contribute more to good 9,9 team management than this supportive handling of your gatekeeping activities.

Receiving the Scheduled Visitor

A scheduled visitor is likely to have a different set of expectations than the uninvited visitor because he or she expects your boss to be fully prepared to make the visit a productive one. This means that you and your boss are ready to deal with the visitor by being ready to respond to and deal with the visitor on the basis of the already established purpose of the visit. Therefore, it is important that you take several steps beforehand.

One is to ensure that your boss has the material necessary to deal with the visitor. He can review it and be well informed as to the meeting agenda, problems to be discussed, and so on. It is also important that you have the names of the visitors in mind so that you can greet them personally and, if appropriate, introduce them by name. Should your boss be unavoidably detained, you need to explain the reasons for his being unavailable. By anticipating such an inconvenience and explaining the reason for it, you ease tensions by providing a framework within which the visitor's expectations for what will occur can be shifted.

Many times you can extend your helpfulness by asking the out-of-town guest whether an airplane reservation can be reconfirmed, a taxi arranged for, or any number of other things the visitor can be assisted in to move efficiently through the visit.

Finally, it may be necessary to summarize and place in the files any decisions made or to deal with follow-up actions. When you have made it possible for the visitor's time to be used efficiently and for the purpose of his or her visit to be dealt with effectively, even though in some cases the results may be negative, you have provided the maximum in consideration for the visitor and in support for your boss.

Dealing with the Uninvited Visitor

Many people come in without making prior arrangements, and their first contact is with you. This is the so-called cold call. Ordinarily it is a salesperson or someone seeking to relate some kind of information that is not easily conveyed over the phone or by correspondence.

This is one of the most difficult assignments for a secretary, especially in the beginning. The best ground rule is to inform the visitor of the company's policy. If the practice is not to arrange a conference for an uninvited visitor, he or she should be told this. The step taken next depends on what the policy is: to check with the boss to see if he is free or to get the visitor's card for a future appointment. In any event, the visitor may expect you to call and let him or her know the next steps, if any.

Preparing for Meetings

Your boss may have frequent meetings. They may be with one or several persons, and they may be formal or informal.

Formal meetings with several people are organized and carried out following prepared agenda. If the boss asks you to be responsible for organizing the agenda, it is a good idea to obtain topics from others who will attend, either by phone or memo, put them in a meaningful order, and then review the order with the boss before making it final. Again, at times it may be necessary to pull files for your boss so that he can be brought up to date on various issues. It is helpful for you to anticipate this, and this is a key area where your planning and thoroughness can aid in setting the tone for a productive meeting.

Keeping a Tickler File

A tickler file, sometimes called a b/f (bring forward) or a b/u (bring up) file, is organized so that it causes you to remember something that you might otherwise forget. If your boss is scheduled to be in Chicago, say, on January 25, several months away, there may be little for him to do immediately with regard to the project because planning for the meeting cannot begin until January 5. You make a note in your tickler file to bring the Chicago meeting scheduled for January 25 to the attention of your boss on January 5. Your tickler file may also contain the topic of the meeting and suggestions regarding files or other data that you should make available to him.

A tickler file can be simple or complex. If simple, it is little more than a reference on a regularly maintained appointment schedule. If complex, an entire system may be set up to correlate the many details involved in forward planning. This file is one of the aids to time management that can help you to arrange work in an orderly manner—freeing you of details to "remember"— and to provide the follow-through so necessary to high-quality performance.

Compiling a Trip Folder

When your boss is away, he may carry documents and supporting materials that are relevant to his trip. Other information that he may carry may be concerned with a travel itinerary, hotels where resevations have been made, telephone calls to clients, and so on.

All of this information comes together in the trip folder. A trip folder is complete when it contains the information the boss needs to work efficiently during his trip. Your ability to anticipate what information needs to be available is key here, and a great deal of material can be developed in advance by setting up a folder as soon as an activity is planned and then adding relevant material along the way. Trip folders are indispensable; they often make the difference between your boss's being able to do a good job and his having difficulty in developing necessary background information.

Many times original documents are placed in the trip folder, but this is done at some risk. The folder itself can be mislaid, or various items may be taken out for use in planning. These may not be returned to the folder. Therefore, it is better to copy materials for the trip folder if at all possible. This keeps the original file intact and at the same time provides the boss with the information necessary to complete his job assignment. When the boss returns the trip folder to you for dismantling, and after he has reviewed with you whatever is pertinent for you to know in order to operate the support system in the period ahead, his trip can be considered completed.

When the Boss Is Away

When the boss is away, it is natural to experience some free time, in which case you may find the day passing slowly. The alternative is to take his absence as an opportunity to work on items that have been left undone. There are almost always things that were put off "until I have more time"—sorting or putting back files, updating the telephone files, reading the long report on company competition, and so on. Using this opportunity to do your own catching up and planning can be invaluable for strengthening your version of the big picture and being able to be on top of details in the future.

You and the Informal System

Your job responsibilities can be mastered, but it takes thoughtful anticipation and flexibility to keep them under control and in perspective. There are many intrusions throughout the day—incoming calls, unannounced visitors, rush completion of projects, and so forth. What we are looking at here is not the number of tasks but the outside demands that take away available time.

Many of these outside demands are the result of interactions with other secretaries, and they can have a great deal of influence on a new secretary. Some secretaries can be excellent sources of information, but you should think carefully before you adopt what other secretaries do as a model for yourself. Doing the same things they do may not be consistent with your best interests.

The same is true of office gossip and personal jealousies. No one can tell you how to deal with these matters, but it is to your advantage to be aware that you may unintentionally commit yourself to participate with the others in these activities. You will also find that these situations can consume a great deal of your time if you do not recognize them for what they are.

Office Security

When you take up a new secretarial assignment, it is wise to ask about the policies of office security. Many bosses maintain locked files and may also lock their desks as well as the office itself. Of course, if you are given keys, you will know there is a policy of office security by which you are expected to abide. It is a good idea to make sure that everything is secure and to lock the office unless your boss remains after you depart.

Summary

Many matters that may be considered administrative routines face every secretary. The objective in this chapter has been to point out how some of these can be dealt with from a 9,9 perspective.

A secretary interacts with a variety of people and faces situations and considerations that are pertinent to her operation of the support system. Inevitably there are phone calls to be placed and phones to be answered, mail to be sorted and letters to be mailed, meetings to be held, scheduled visitors to receive and uninvited visitors to be dealt with, and interactions with other secretaries. There are issues of office schedules, taking breaks, lunch hours, and so on. Dealing soundly with these matters is the goal of a secretary operating in a 9,9 orientation. Many details of office routine can be cleared up by means of a straightforward question to the boss. Solutions to other problems become evident through experience. Still other questions can be answered by secretaries who have been with the organization for a period of time. Thoroughness, planning, time management, and dealing with the expectations of others, including your boss, are at the heart of operating an effective support system.

10
Your Grid Style and Your Boss's

Just as is true for yourself, your boss has a primary Grid style and a backup Grid style, and it is important for you to be aware of them. If you are aware of his habitual methods of working with you, you are in a better position to respond in ways that will promote positive cooperation.

There is another situation to consider here. With the introduction of word processing centers, the secretary has been freed from a great many routine typing activities. This makes it possible for her to support more than one boss. Supporting more than one boss places increased demands on her for scheduling appointments, dealing with invited and uninvited guests, representing her boss(es) to others, and so on. All of this places a premium on the skills that have been emphasized in this book.

This multiple-boss system also opens up a variety of possibilities for misunderstandings between her boss(es) and herself. Boss A may feel she is giving more support to Boss B, C, or D than to him. Boss B may never seem to do anything for himself and therefore takes more of her time than he deserves, whereas Boss C is the picture of cooperation, doing things for himself he might reasonably expect her to do. Beyond these complex issues, the secretary risks being drawn into management politics by talking to Boss C about her frustrations with Boss B, carrying a tale from Boss A to Boss D, and spreading tensions in other ways. Therefore, a multiple-boss secretarial support system will require an even greater use of 9,9 secretarial skills than is demanded in the one-boss/one-secretary system.

Now let's examine the boss's styles. The grid figure depicting these managerial styles is presented in Figure 3.

Figure 3. The Managerial Grid

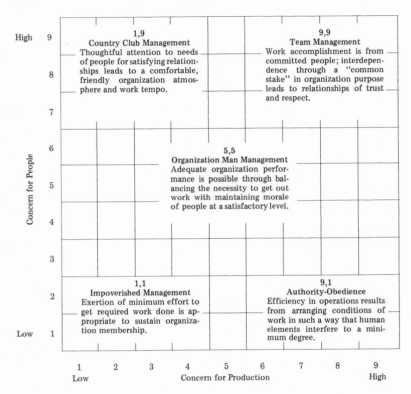

High 9 — **1,9** Country Club Management — Thoughtful attention to needs of people for satisfying relationships leads to a comfortable, friendly organization atmosphere and work tempo.

9,9 Team Management — Work accomplishment is from committed people; interdependence through a "common stake" in organization purpose leads to relationships of trust and respect.

5,5 Organization Man Management Adequate organization performance is possible through balancing the necessity to get out work with maintaining morale of people at a satisfactory level.

1,1 Impoverished Management Exertion of minimum effort to get required work done is appropriate to sustain organization membership.

9,1 Authority-Obedience Efficiency in operations results from arranging conditions of work in such a way that human elements interfere to a minimum degree.

Concern for People — High 9, 8, 7, 6, 5, 4, 3, 2, Low 1

1   2   3   4   5   6   7   8   9
Low   Concern for Production   High

Source: Robert R. Blake and Jane S. Mouton, "A Framework for Assessing Managerial Orientations" (Austin, Texas: Scientific Methods, Inc., 1964), p. 2. Reproduced by permission.

It is often difficult to know how to deal with a boss regarding his Grid style. You have the option of adjusting to his Grid style. In other words, if your boss's basic Grid style is a 9,1 orientation, you can deal with him the same way. (If he growls at you, you growl back.) Or you may respond to him in your own way to his 9,1 orientation. One common reaction is to become a doormat and let your boss walk all over you while you feel hurt inside, or to withdraw into your shell in order to give him the indication that his treatment doesn't bother you. Or you may deal with your boss by responding in a 9,9-oriented manner, whatever his Grid style may be. The evidence indicates that when you interact with your boss in a 9,9-oriented way, you have a greater likelihood of success, regardless of what his Grid style may be. However, it is most productive to be able to accept the growl for what it is, that is, unpleasant behavior, and to respond by giving the boss the kind of support that a 9,9-oriented secretary is capable of providing. The interesting discovery is that if you do not growl back (in a 9,1 way), or act as a doormat (in a 1,9 way), or withdraw into your shell (in a 1,1 way), you will soon find that your boss makes an exception and treats you with courtesy and respect. In this case, you are making a positive contribution to the organization as well as supporting your boss by increasing the likelihood of his becoming more effective.

Not all bosses have a 9,1 orientation, of course, and to help you develop the diagnostic skills needed to determine your boss's Grid style, as well as secretary Grid styles, examples are provided in the rest of this chapter. Make a judgment as to which Grid styles are represented by the boss and the secretary and write down your answers. The answers and rationale for them are provided in order for you to check your skill in seeing what is going on in the situations. In addition, how a 9,9-oriented secretary might deal with each boss is described in order to provide insights into more effective ways of developing a sound boss-secretary relationship.

Example 1

Gina has been Mr. Burt's secretary for about four years. Ten years ago he was recruited to run a large organization's Executive Development program. Gina knows how important his career is to him and has marveled at the way his career has developed. They are talking about an important meeting held yesterday that was attended by a number of senior executives who reviewed the training department's activities for the past year and the programs to be conducted for the year ahead.

Mr. Burt:	All right if I say something about the meeting yesterday?
Gina:	Yes, of course.
Mr. Burt:	I mean, don't take this as personal criticism, although it is rather important.
Gina:	What is it? Is something wrong? Did I offend someone somehow?
Mr. Burt:	No. At least not anything serious. But . . . now, how shall I put it? There are two worlds for a boss and his secretary. One is when we are in my office and can talk about anything in an informal way. The other is when we are in public, and then we have to be, well, more formal.
Gina:	But I want to help you whenever I can. Surely there is no harm in showing it. I admire the excellent record that you have established in the company.
Mr. Burt:	Well, it doesn't sound right to make people feel you are paying me too many compliments. There were some pretty envious people in the meeting, you know.
Gina:	I'd never have thought so. They all seem so . . . nice.
Mr. Burt:	They know how to conduct themselves. They don't embarrass one another in a public meeting, of course, but that doesn't mean they're not angry under the surface.
Gina:	I'm sorry. Did I really embarrass you?
Mr. Burt:	Well, when you were talking with Mr. Bell. . . .
Gina:	Oh, yes, Mr. Bell. He's such a nice gentleman. I'm so glad he's your boss. He thanked me for my concern for your success.

Mr. Burt:	You should think before you say anything to people like Bell. For instance, when he asked you where you were from, you said Newark.
Gina:	Why, sure. That's where I grew up.
Mr. Burt:	It might have sounded better if you had said New York. I'm not knocking Newark, but. . . .
Gina:	Oh, I'm sorry—I'll do that next time.
Mr. Burt:	And when he asked you where you went to college, you said that I had gone to Harvard but that you never went at all.
Gina:	I only meant to emphasize that you were the genius in this company. I was boosting you. What does it matter? Why are you. . . ?
Mr. Burt:	What does it matter? It matters a great deal in this corporation. Bell and most of the other executives and their secretaries are college graduates. The more you have in common with them, the more they like you. Gina, please try to think when you are in these situations. You're enrolled for the NYU Sunrise Semester on TV. You could have said you were taking social anthropology at New York University.
Gina:	I'll remember that next time. I do want them to accept me.

What Grid style do you see in the interaction of Mr. Burt and Gina?

The Grid style of Mr. Burt is _____.
The Grid style of Gina is _____.

In this interaction we see many indications that Mr. Burt's Grid style is in the 5,5 orientation. Among them is the apologetic way in which he brings up the topic, indirectly asking Gina's permission to approach the subject. He speaks of his embarrassment at the compliments paid by her and of her warmth and sweetness with Bell, his boss. He shows other aspects of the 5,5 orientation when he indicates that New York is more sophisticated than Newark, that being a college graduate is important, and that taking a course at NYU shows an obvious inclination for learning. His approach is one of concern for status, prestige, protocol, and appearances. Mr. Burt's fear is that Gina may have overplayed her hand on one side of the social protocol and underplayed it on the other.

We see that Gina's basic Grid style is in the 1,9 orientation. She is so eager to bring attention to her boss that she goes beyond what might be considered appropriate. This is seen in the comment about where her boss went to college and in the compliments she pays him about his achievements. The other side of her 1,9 orientation becomes evident when she apparently feels terrible about embarrassing him.

Had Gina's orientation been in the 9,9 direction, most likely she would not have become involved in a situation that required a double standard for communication: a private informal one and a public formal one. Instead, she would have acted toward Mr. Burt in a manner that is appropriate both in their office discussions and in her public activities as his secretary.

While she would feel free to speak well of Mr. Burt simply as a matter of respect for him, it is likely that she would have considered it improper to praise him in order to let others know how wonderful she thinks he is. In addition, she would be aware of the underlying antagonisms among the several executives and would have avoided saying things that could create deeper antagonisms.

We see also Mr. Burt tutoring Gina in how to interpret the truth so that things look better than they are. It is doubtful that a 9,9-oriented secretary would respond favorably to such a suggestion. She might simply point out that facts are facts and that it is better to live with them than to violate basic rules of candor in order to create an inaccurate impression.

Regarding Gina's and Mr. Burt's discussing the importance of status and how Gina might respond in ways to promote her acceptance in the eyes of others, a 9,9-oriented secretary would be inclined to seek respect and the acceptance that follows on the basis of her competence in carrying out her responsibilities.

It is difficult to imagine Mr. Burt thanking a 9,9-oriented secretary for her concern about his success. On the other hand, we can sense that Mr. Burt might acknowledge his appreciation for Gina's involvement in her work and her commitment to the activities for which their office is responsible.

Example 2

Mr. Graham returns from a meeting. Dorothy starts the conversation.

Dorothy: Have a good meeting with the boss?

Mr. Graham: Not bad. He said good morning to me when I came in. I didn't find out where I am heading promotion-wise, but I guess I ought not to be worried. He says I'm steady and at least I don't push.

Dorothy: Guess what? I've decided to give myself that camera I have been looking at so long for my birthday.

Mr. Graham: Oh. I saw you reading microwave ads so I thought you were saving toward a microwave oven.

Dorothy: No. I've changed my mind.

Mr. Graham: Any calls or messages while I was out?

Dorothy: Just a note from Craig. He wants a pay raise again.

Mr. Graham: Yeah. He thinks money grows on trees. He should have gone to the school of hard knocks like I did.

Dorothy:	Well, he's still a kid. He'll learn.
Mr. Graham:	I expect you're right. Live and let live is what they say.
Dorothy:	Okay if I leave early? I've got some shopping to do.
Mr. Graham:	Well, I might as well too.

The Grid style of Mr. Graham is ―――.
The Grid style of Dorothy is ―――.

Mr. Graham has gravitated into a 1,1 orientation. Dorothy seems to have adopted the same approach. Mr. Graham's 1,1 orientation is evident in his low-key, shallow conversation. Dorothy seems to have no reluctance to tell him that instead of working while he was out, she was planning a purchase. The same attitude comes through when she says she would like to leave early and he says, "Me too." These two are congenial enough to one another, but neither seems very concerned about the company or about contributing to its success.

It's a case of two people who have gravitated into the same Grid style: 1,1/1,1.

If Dorothy's approach had been in the 9,9 direction, she might have asked Mr. Graham if he had had a good meeting with the boss, but only as a formality, not as a basis for having a conversation with Mr. Graham about what transpired in the meeting. And Mr. Graham's remark about where he is headed promotion-wise would have been inappropriate in a sound boss-secretary relationship. The rest of the conversation (e.g., about purchasing a camera or a microwave) is equally time-wasting between boss and secretary.

The final point to be made about this conversation is related to Dorothy's asking Mr. Graham if she can leave early to do her shopping. A 9,9-oriented secretary would leave early only under circumstances where personal considerations made it imperative and under conditions where any boss would regard her request as legitimate.

Paul Lock is discussing a recent marketing project with his secretary, Rita.

Example 3

Mr. Lock:	I thought we weren't going to do a third follow-up on that list of prospects.
Rita:	I had second thoughts about it. We're not talking about much money and another printing might produce some business.
Mr. Lock:	You shouldn't make a decision like that without consulting me!
Rita:	I don't know why you're getting upset. I said it's not much expense. Your budget can stand it. Besides, you were out. . . .
Mr. Lock:	That's not the point! I have never authorized you to make that kind of decision.
Rita:	Let me finish. You were out of the office when I made that decision. Which reminds me, you're always out of the office. If you would stay in half the time, I wouldn't have to do your job and mine, too! So excuse me, I'm going to coffee. . . .

The Grid style of Mr. Lock is _____.

The Grid style of Rita is _____.

Mr. Lock and Rita speak from mutual antagonism and anger characteristic of two people who interact according to a 9,1 orientation. Both quickly become defensive and accusatory. Rita wins by getting up and leaving.

Were Rita 9,9-oriented, it is unlikely that such mutual antagonism would have had the opportunity to develop. She would learn more about Mr. Lock's rationale for his way of doing things. Through critique she could influence his thinking about sound decisions. This would preclude Rita's exercising unilateral judgment, as we see her doing in this discussion. Furthermore, if Mr. Lock were away on business and it became an urgent matter for such a decision to be made, she would have sufficient rationale and background to make it herself, or she could contact him to get his reactions.

Also, should a disagreement between herself and Mr. Lock arise, Rita would use it as an opportunity to confront their differences and to explore the underlying causes in order to relieve them, rather than leave Mr. Lock fuming.

Example 4

Billie has taken notes at a meeting Mr. Crow presided over.

Billie:	You were great. It was amazing the way the others came around to your point of view after you spoke your mind.
Mr. Crow:	Well, it had gotten to the point where I just couldn't put up with Bill's dogmatism any longer. He didn't understand what was really at stake, and he had misrepresented the basic position of our R&D effort as to the best balance between basic and applied research. That's what did it.
Billie:	I like to listen to you debate. You're very eloquent.
Mr. Crow:	Did it come through clearly? You understood what I was saying? Did all my points check out with what you know about the problem? Which points didn't?
Billie:	It was really marvelous. I wish I could express myself the way you do.

The Grid style of Mr. Crow is _____.

The Grid style of Billie is _____.

Billie is talking to Mr. Crow from a 1,9 orientation, complimenting him by pointing out his talent in bringing others around to his point of view. She gains self-appreciation by approving of him. She indicates her pleasure in listening to him debate and her appreciation of his eloquence, and then adds; "I wish I could express myself the way you do."

Mr. Crow's approach is 9,9. He relates to others in such a way as to exert influence on their points of view. He is unprepared to tolerate dogmatism. He feels that the misrepresentation was based on an unbalanced view of the situation, and therefore it was his obligation to reconstruct the situation on a more objective basis. Furthermore, he probes beneath the surface of Billie's compliments to check on the understandability and validity of the points he made. She simply continues the compliments.

If Mr. Crow's 9,9 Grid orientation had been deeper, he would have continued the discussion and not let Billie's commentary remain limited to compliments. He might have said, "Billie, I'm pleased you liked it, but can you think of *any* points that I made that contradict what you know? Let's talk about that." In this way he would be encouraging Billie to offer a critique, and he would be gaining the benefits of her perceptiveness, instead of simply letting her try to cement their relationship through her positive reactions. If Billie had a 9,9-oriented perspective, she would have listened to the meeting from the vantage point of her responsibility to give her boss genuine feedback on how he came across, on others' reactions to his arguments, and so on. She would not have hesitated to give him valid feedback.

Example 5

The boss has returned to his office after his annual physical checkup.

Mr. Nelson:	The doc really read me the riot act.
Marie:	Oh? What did he find?
Mr. Nelson:	My ticker is still okay and the chest x-rays are negative, but my weight. . . .
Marie:	But you're not overweight. You rarely even leave the office for a snack.
Mr. Nelson:	Yes, but I want to talk about the donuts and cake you always bring to the coffee room. You're the one causing me to be overweight.
Marie:	But I like you to be in a good mood.
Mr. Nelson:	Well, if you want to know the truth, I told him you're getting chubby too.
Marie:	Oh, how could you say that! Surely it's not dangerous to be a little plump.
Mr. Nelson:	Come on, face it, Marie. I've said I would co-operate, and you've promised time and again to get donuts out of the coffee room. The next donut I see goes into the trash.
Marie:	When you're hungry and irritable, you get cross with me and everybody else. I want you to be pleasant to be around.
Mr. Nelson:	So I have to run a health risk just to keep you happy? I don't run a social club around here, you know.

The Grid style of Mr. Nelson is _____.
The Grid style of Marie is _____.

Mr. Nelson puts the blame for his failure to maintain his weight on Marie. He accuses her of reneging on a promise to cut out donuts. Marie tells us that criticism of her behavior causes her to feel rejected. These are such painful feelings that she will do whatever she must to avoid having them. In this case, the relationship is 9,1/1,9, with the boss a person who can lash out and the secretary someone who cannot tolerate such destructive behavior.

Were Marie 9,9-oriented, she would say, "I didn't realize that you see donuts as the cause of your overweight problem. One solution is that I stop bringing donuts, but you might also consider not indulging. What do you think?" Had this been said, it might have resulted in a further bit of combat, but it might also have brought Mr. Nelson to the realization that snacks and coffee-break activities are a personal matter over which the boss need not exercise supervisory control in his own personal interests.

Example 6

Nina and her boss are talking after a conference he has had with his boss in which he was criticized for failing to deal with the problem of two subordinates whose competitiveness with one another has reached a destructive level.

Nina:	I saw this problem coming up and I thought I brought it to your attention.
Mr. Dale:	Yes, you mentioned it. But I didn't think it had the serious impact that you implied it had and that the boss insists it has.
Nina:	Look, you always seem to want me to protect you so that you can live without any problems, frictions, or strains.
Mr. Dale:	I'm not sure that's fair. Surely we can be nice to each other. Kind words help a lot, you know.
Nina:	I want to shield you from problems, but you've got to help. I can't tell you all's well at eight o'clock, nine o'clock, ten o'clock, and so on through the day.
Mr. Dale:	But your friendliness means something to me. I know you're a strong person. I've always put you high on that dimension. You're also smart. I've said again and again that I've often taken

	actions that I didn't want to take simply because you thought it was important for me to do so.
Nina:	Yes, that's true. I don't mind your leaning on me, but it's a management responsibility to see these things and to take effective action on them. I enjoy thinking about these matters, and when I do, I really want you to give them attention.
Mr. Dale:	Well, yes, my feeling is that everything is pretty much okay if you don't find something negative in the situation. It gives me a sense of well-being not to have to keep myself in a state of vigilance.
Nina:	I really do think that this problem is more serious than you seem to think. You must act now. If I were you, I would call Joe. . . .
Mr. Dale:	*(on telephone)* Hello, Mary. Is Joe there?

The Grid style of Mr. Dale is ———.
The Grid style of Nina is ———.

Mr. Dale has just been reprimanded by his own boss for allowing a bad situation to develop between two of his subordinates. He finds it difficult to deal with conflict. Nina had drawn his attention to this problem in the past. He is now almost pleading with her to continue to exercise strength in his behalf.

Nina is bothered that her boss hasn't acted on her advice. But she is patient and persistent and promises to give him her help if he'll do his part.

Mr. Dale's Grid style is in the 1,9 orientation while Nina is approaching this problem from a maternalistic orientation.

It probably would have been difficult for a 9,9-oriented secretary to have been of much help at this point. Certainly, this protecting of Mr. Dale has contributed to his weakness, not aided him in developing strength.

Nina could have asked earlier—whenever the problem

arose—about other courses of action that Mr. Dale might have considered instead of letting the problem grow. In this way she would have been a good sounding board for him to test possibilities and see approaches that he might otherwise have been unaware of.

The real person to help Mr. Dale is the line boss. He might confront Mr. Dale directly about his tendency to yield or smooth things over whenever conflict arises and help him to see the adverse consequences of not facing up. This support from his boss could be of much benefit for Mr. Dale's managerial strength. A confrontation by Nina is less appropriate than the same confrontation by Mr. Dale's boss would be.

Example 7

Diane and her boss, Mr. Franks, are discussing things in general.

Mr. Franks: It seems to me that kids nowadays probably are not very much different from kids two thousand or more years ago. Why, even Aristotle complained about their lack of respect and how they wanted to go against society. Maybe there is too much attention given to them and too much concern with new young employees.

Diane: Yes, and in that way of thinking you're in agreement with Jack Dawson. He does write good presidential editorials in our newsletter, doesn't he? About young employees and how to help them become good corporate citizens.

Mr. Franks: Well, I've been thinking a lot about that recently, what with Bill getting out of college and going to work next year.

Diane: Have you talked with Jack Dawson about your opinions?

Mr. Franks: Huh?

Diane:	If he knew you were thinking about the same issues in much the same way, it would prove how close he is with the man on the street, and he would be very pleased to know this.
Mr. Franks:	Yes. I feel quite sure that he is right.
Diane:	The editorials on the president's page are the most talked about in the whole newsletter.
Mr. Franks:	Even more than the athletics . . . Dawson, he's been a good president for this company.
Diane:	All the secretaries in the other offices think his editorials are good too, and they tell their bosses. I suspect that they pass the word up to Mr. Dawson.
Mr. Franks:	It's really great to have a president with such a broad vision, a person so concerned about the well-being of everyone in this company.
Diane:	That's partly why we are all so proud to work here.

The Grid style of Mr. Franks is ———.
The Grid style of Diane is ———.

The conversation provides a good illustration of how attitudes of people in a company converge toward one another. The conversation isn't deep, and when we are told that everyone is reading Dawson's material and many or most of the members repeat his thinking more or less as a catechism, we know that a 5,5 orientation is evident between the boss and the secretary.

A 9,9-oriented secretary might question the extent to which the attitudes of young people now are rooted in historical values. The president's referring to Greek history may be a way of avoiding coming to grips with current realities. Diane could ask Mr. Franks what he thinks about these matters, and her questions might help him to become aware of the origins of his own attitudes and to decide whether they should be so loyally anchored to those of the corporate president or whether other factors should receive consideration in his attitudes toward new employees.

Example 8

Mr. Reed and Jennifer, his newly employed, inexperienced secretary, are reviewing how he prefers his telephone calls to be handled and how to greet visitors.

Mr. Reed:	By answering the phone as outlined, you've proved to me that you are paying attention to my directions. I like that. Compliance is the first step; without that, no learning is possible.
Jennifer:	Thank you. That makes me feel better.
Mr. Reed:	Now, let's move on. I want to tell you how to greet a visitor. Stop whatever you're doing. Give it your undivided attention. Begin by asking, "Good morning. This is Mr. Reed's office. May I be of help?"
Jennifer:	May I ask a question?
Mr. Reed:	Yes, go ahead.
Jennifer:	I'm not sure how to solve the problem when the phone rings just as the visitor opens the door.
Mr. Reed:	That's where judgment must be relied on, but here's the basic rule: Give precedence to the one you are already dealing with. If the phone rings before the visitor arrives, the caller gets your priority. If the visitor arrives before the phone rings, the visitor gets your priority.
Jennifer:	Sounds complex and difficult. Most people don't like to be kept waiting.
Mr. Reed:	That's the test of a good receptionist. If you try, you'll develop the ability to do it inoffensively and respectfully. I have confidence in you.
Jennifer:	I will work to prove I deserve it.

Mr. Reed:	I'm sure you'll do well because you listen and accept directions.
Jennifer:	Thanks.

The Grid style of Mr. Reed is ———.
The Grid style of Jennifer is ———.

Mr. Reed's orientation is paternalistic. He carefully takes Jennifer through each step of how he wants the phone/visitor interface handled. And he rewards her with such comments as "I like that. Compliance is the first step . . . ," which indicates that if she performs well, she will be rewarded with praise. Another example is his extension of assurance: "I'm sure you'll do well," followed by the contingency "because you listen and accept directions." If she does not perform well, then most likely she will experience his displeasure.

Jennifer asks questions that imply a 9,9 orientation. She could have chosen to simply sit and do as instructed, or to warmly accept Mr. Reed's instructions so as not to risk any disharmony. Jennifer was direct and to the point: "May I ask a question?" "What if the phone rings just as the visitor opens the door?" which expresses her willingness to learn and her desire to know the facts.

Even though her orientation appears to have a 9,9 quality to it, toward the end of the conversation Jennifer yields to his paternalism when she responds to his confidence in her ability: "I will work to prove that I deserve it."

At this point, she might have said the following, and the discussion could have continued in another vein.

Jennifer:	May I ask a question?
Mr. Reed:	Certainly.
Jennifer:	What do you do when you are in a conference with someone and you receive a call from the president?

Mr. Reed:	I immediately respond to whatever it is that the president wants. He is the top of the hierarchy, you know.
Jennifer:	That's interesting because the basic rule does not hold under the circumstance, does it?
Mr. Reed:	You're quite right. The basic rule is a good one, but there are numerous exceptions and this is one of the important ones.
Jennifer:	What would you want me to do when I am dealing with a visitor and the president drops by while you are in conference? Should I tell him that you are tied up, or would you want me to interrupt you so that you could deal with him?
Mr. Reed:	You're posing very difficult choices. I think this is a very good topic; perhaps we can set aside some time later this afternoon to talk more about it.
Jennifer:	I would like that very much. It would certainly help me with these kinds of dilemmas.

Were Jennifer to have done this, she would have extended her 9,9 orientation by opening Mr. Reed's eyes to his mechanical way of giving her categorical rules, which in fact apply only in certain circumstances.

Example 9

Mr. Cole is meeting with Jocelyn to discuss her progress in the past three weeks.

Mr. Cole:	I think your work is very satisfactory, Jocelyn. What are your reactions to the last three weeks?
Jocelyn:	I have the routine under control now. Mr. Wood's secretary, Betty, has been very helpful to me.
Mr. Cole:	Yes, Betty is a thoughtful person and she shows

	good judgment in hiring personnel, but I'm always ready to help you when needed. By the way, how is Bob doing in graduate school?
Jocelyn:	Fine. He hopes to graduate in about a year. If I can keep working, I think we can pull it off financially. If you're saying I'm now on permanent status, that's certainly good news.
Mr. Cole:	Consider yourself permanent . . . my right hand. I think I'll tell Betty now you're all mine. What do you think of that?
Jocelyn:	Well, I . . . uh . . . thank you, but Betty and I have a good working relationship . . .
Mr. Cole:	Fine, fine, not that you need to rely on me . . . but after all, I do sign the paychecks. *(laughs)* Now, are you coming to the company party Saturday night? I'll take you around. Maybe we can get to know each other better then.
Jocelyn:	Mr. Cole, I need this job badly, but I think you should understand that I intend to do my duties as your private secretary in a businesslike manner.
Mr. Cole:	*(slightly taken aback)* Oh, I'm sorry if you misunderstood. All I meant was that I wanted you to feel at home here.

The Grid style of Mr. Cole is _____.
The Grid style of Jocelyn is _____.

Obviously Mr. Cole has waited until Jocelyn has accepted permanent status before coming on strong. Mr. Cole puts out tentative feelers of the 5,5-oriented sort that have harassment overtones. He avoids embarrassment by backing off when it is evident that she is not responding in kind. He also proclaims his interest in her is only as an employee of the company.

Jocelyn, operating in a 9,9 orientation, reads the situation quickly and confronts him by leaving no doubt as to what she sees her obligations to be. She is willing to risk losing her job by being open and candid but hopes they can arrive at a mutual understanding.

She has taken the initiative to set the standard of conduct between them, and we see that he is aware of that standard. She could act in an even more 9,9-oriented manner by concluding the conversation with, "Yes, I am coming to the party and Bob will also. I want you to meet him. I think you will find him a very interesting person." In this way she could have conveyed to Mr. Cole that her friendly feelings toward him had not been injured—through closing the circle by bringing her husband into the picture and by doing so in a proper manner.

Example 10

It's 9:15 A.M. and Mr. Neeley is reviewing the day's schedule with his secretary, Norene.

Mr. Neeley: Well, what's in store for me today, Norene?

Norene: At ten you're scheduled to attend the meeting on long-range planning.

Mr. Neeley: As far as I'm concerned, that's a yearly meeting that should roll around every five years. It's all just talk, talk, talk.

Norene: That may be true, but you know you have to go. It's required. And I'll type up your reactions to the meeting and get them in to the president quickly, just as he likes it.

Mr. Neeley: Still, you would think Davis would have figured out how to run the show by now.

Norene: I'm sure Mr. Davis knows what he is doing. You are well advised to go along and support what is required if you're going to stay in his good graces.

Mr. Neeley: I guess you're right. After the meeting, though, cancel the afternoon's schedule. I'm going to hit a few golf balls.

Norene: No, I want you to come back here first and give me the rundown so I can type the report. Then you can leave.

The Grid style of Mr. Neeley is _____.
The Grid style of Norene is _____.

Norene takes care of Mr. Neeley in a maternalistic fashion. This suits his 1,1 orientation, which is evidenced by his lack of interest in the meeting or even in completing a day's work for that matter. To secure her own position, Norene makes sure he stays in good graces with the boss by getting the report in quickly. If he is a good boy and does his part, "come back here first," then she'll take care of covering for him by finishing the report.

Exercising her responsibilities in a more 9,9 fashion, Norene might be more helpful by aiding Mr. Neeley to explore the consequences of his indifferent attitude. When Mr. Neeley says, "It's all just talk, talk, talk," Norene might ask, "Mr. Neeley, have you had the occasion to discuss your perceptions of these planning meetings with the president?" Mr. Neeley might respond with, "No, what's the use?" or "He wouldn't listen," or "It doesn't matter anyway." Or he might say, "No, I haven't."

Norene might continue the conversation by asking the following: "Would it be appropriate for you to do so?" "Would it be helpful to the president to know your attitude?" "How do you think he might react if he were aware that you think the meetings are a waste of time?" Any of these might help Mr. Neeley to see the impoverished character of his own motivations.

The same is true with regard to Norene's preparing the notes for the president. She might say, "How do you want me to deal with the notes that the president expects me to prepare? If you are absent this afternoon, it will not be possible for me to make them available to him." She might also say, "On one occasion I didn't get them to the president's secretary until four o'clock and she called for an explanation. That may not happen again, but if it does, I would like your instruction as to what explanation you want me to offer."

These are relatively strong initiatives for a secretary to take, yet they are within the legitimate bounds of conducting a support system that aids a boss to become more aware of the consequences of his own inactions.

Summary

This chapter has shown the way to analyze boss and secretary Grid styles through illustrations of a range of secretary-boss situations. It has also suggested how a 9,9-oriented secretary might deal with each of the situations described. These illustrations of 9,9 behavior also showed how a 9,9-oriented secretary can exercise initiative without producing antagonisms and hostility, and made clear the important contribution that she as the leader of the office support system can make.

A secretary has three options for dealing with her boss. She can reflect his Grid orientation (for example, respond in a 9,1 way to a 9,1-oriented boss). Or she can adopt a complementary Grid style (for example, respond with sweetness and light of the 1,9 sort to a 9,1-oriented boss). Another option is to respond to him, whatever his Grid style, in a 9,9 orientation. This is by no means easy to do, but when it is done, it is very rewarding. Exhibiting this kind of behavior is certainly the strongest contribution a secretary can make in helping her boss become more mature and effective and in helping the organization become more successful. When two people, regardless of rank, can get the job done well without falling back on authority, this can be taken as an indication of good, solid 9,9-oriented teamwork.

11
Your Self-Development

You completed a Grid mirror in Chapter 2. What you saw can now be analyzed and interpreted in terms of Grid theories that have been presented. First, you may want to reexamine the rankings you made at that time and to adjust them now that you have a more thorough understanding of the Grid. Use the same self-evaluation questions you used in Chapter 2 for *re*ranking the elements. Then record your new rankings in Figure 4, just as you did in Chapter 2. Now what Grid style do you see as typical of yourself? Are you predominantly 9,9? Or 9,1; 1,9; 1,1; or 5,5? If what you saw was 9,9, is that the real you?

Note again that self-deception may have occurred when you

Figure 4. Tally of second self-evaluation rankings on Grid elements.

Element	Grid Style					
	1,1	*1,9*	*5,5*	*9,1*	*Maternalism*	*9,9*
1. Decisions	A1__	B1__	C1__	D1__	E1_____	F1__
2. Convictions	A2__	B2__	C2__	D2__	E2_____	F2__
3. Conflict	A3__	B3__	C3__	D3__	E3_____	F3__
4. Emotions	A4__	B4__	C4__	D4__	E4_____	F4__
5. Thoroughness	A5__	B5__	C5__	D5__	E5_____	F5__
6. Enthusiasm	A6__	B6__	C6__	D6__	E6_____	F6__
TOTAL	A__	B__	C__	D__	E_____	F__

made your rankings because it is difficult to distinguish between what "sounds good" and what is an accurate self-description. The deception results from people's tendency to confuse the way they *want to be* with the way they *are*. Although it is very difficult to achieve objectivity in self-description, it is very important to try.

However, a secretary may be unable to view her behavior objectively and accurately. She may fool herself, saying her approach is 9,9 when it really is 9,1. Or she may confuse 5,5 organization attitudes with 9,9-oriented team achievement. She may rationalize that a 1,9 orientation of sweetness and light really gets everyone involved. She may even delude herself into believing that a 1,1 orientation is the right way to settle back and emotionally quit when she looks at all the problems she must contend with.

These rationalizations are caused by many background factors. Among them is the fact that many people simply have not had the opportunity to reflect and to develop a thoughtful view as to what constitutes sound behavior. As a result, whatever they have learned from parents, teachers, or friends is accepted more or less at face value and relied on without being subjected to critical evaluation. The fact that some of what has been learned may contradict other aspects of what has been learned is not readily apparent to the person, and therefore, without realizing it, she can embrace contradictory notions at different times. This is really a very significant problem. For example, we know that 70 percent of managers see themselves as 9,9 prior to attending a seminar on the Managerial Grid.* This figure drops to 20 percent once self-deception has been stripped away.

Having completed your self-assessment, you are now in a position to take a further step to corroborate the conclusions you have reached. After you have developed hypotheses as to (1) your dominant orientation, (2) your backup orientation, and (3)

---

*Scientific Methods, Inc., P.O. Box 195, Austin, Texas, conducts seminars on the Managerial Grid worldwide and seminars on the Secretary Grid in many United States locations, as well as on an in-house basis.

how extreme these orientations are, you can evaluate your findings by asking your boss and others to describe how they see you. They too can picture you by completing the element study in Chapter 2.

Can You Change?

A popular saying is, "Life begins at 40." On the other hand, many people reach a certain age, perhaps even younger than 40, and they stay there—at least in their minds. In other words, some people become complacent, stuck in a rut, and very resistant to change. Whether life begins at 40 or stops at 30 has little to do with bones, muscles, or nerves. It has everything to do with a person's point of view. An individual can get crusty and dead from the neck up at 20 or can be lively, creative, enthusiastic, and growing professionally at 60 and older. It is now realized that people's capacity for new learning continues over their entire career and even after they have stopped working. The problem is not in the capacity to learn but in the attitude toward learning. When attitudes toward learning are positive, learning is never ending. Let's assume a positive attitude toward learning and see where it leads us.

Learning by Making Comparisons

Conditions are favorable for learning whenever you can make comparisons between two or more possible actions. Then you can examine the actions' similarities and differences, analyze the reasons for them, and determine which of them will likely lead to the best outcome. When you can do all this, you are in a position to plot a course of action that will take you from where you are to where you want to be.

Take this concept of how learning occurs and apply it to changing your Grid style, if that is what you want to do, or to strengthening the one you have, if that is your choice. First, the Grid itself provides the basis for a series of comparisons. In many different ways, as you have read this book, you have been comparing a 9,9 orientation with the other styles of behavior. You can see the similarities and differences in the 9,1 and the 9,9 orientations. One is that both have a high concern for getting results. A 9,1-oriented secretary disregards the other person as a unique individual, while a 9,9 approach appreciates the individual as worthy of respect. This is a key difference.

There are also similarities and differences in the 1,9 and 1,1 orientations. Neither has much concern for getting results, but a secretary with a 1,9 attitude enjoys people as people, while the 1,1-oriented secretary is indifferent to them. A 5,5-oriented secretary is shallow and mechanical, while a 9,9 one is deep and committed.

Testing Your Understanding of Grid Concepts

A first step in strengthening yourself is to possess a clear understanding of Grid concepts. Here is how you can test yourself. Take a particular situation you are currently facing and write down what the 9,1 approach toward that situation would be. Then describe the 1,9 attitude. Now write down the 1,1 reaction. How would a 5,5-oriented secretary think about the situation? Finally, picture the 9,9 approach to dealing with it.

You may then want to switch back to parts of this book that relate to similar situations and test your statements against the text. You may want to change some of your statements and simply refine others. You will find that writing these statements will help you to identify various ways of seeing a situation and, therefore, of dealing with it. If you continue to do this from time to time, your understanding of the Grid will increase, as will your ability to analyze a situation and choose the best response to it because you will be able to see alternative ways of dealing with the situation that might differ from your usual approach.

Comparing Your Own Attitude and Behavior with the Grid

You can compare and analyze similarities and differences among the five major orientations, but, of course, there is a far more important comparison to make if you want to change or strengthen yourself. This involves examining your own attitudes and behavior in terms of the Grid and identifying the Grid orientation that corresponds most closely with your own. This will tell you where you are. You did this earlier with the elements.

A second step is to come to your own conclusions as to why you are there and to decide whether this is where you want to be. In making your decision, you will find it helpful to analyze the Grid styles that are not at all like you; this will tell you something about your aversions. Once you understand what it is you dislike and why you dislike it, you may very well want to ask yourself if you interact poorly with other individuals whose Grid styles are opposite to your own. You may come to see why some people bother you, and you can discover new ways of working more effectively with people who represent aspects of behavior that you dislike. The chances are that once you understand your own feelings and actions, you will be able to work more constructively and positively with all people.

Choosing the Ideal Style

There is still another way that you can use the Grid as the basis for self-development. It involves identifying the Grid style that fits your ideal. Go even further. Identify the soundest backup you can adopt and the type of situation that would impel you to use it. Knowing the Grid description that currently fits you—as you have been operating—and knowing the Grid style that would make you the most effective provide a foundation on which you can set development objectives for yourself. In making this comparison between the actual you and the ideal you, you will be able to see what you do that is sound and what you do that is not. You will also increase your awareness of what you need to do in order to act in a sounder way.

Let's assume that you selected the 9,9 orientation as the ideal, for this is the most likely possibility. Note that no matter how sound any particular Grid style you chose might seem to be, it is a realistic choice only insofar as it is workable. Even though the 9,9 orientation is a practical, problem-solving approach that you are probably capable of adopting and is one to which most persons can respond favorably, there are situations in which a 9,9 orientation—or any style you adopt as the soundest—may be unworkable. You may not have sufficient skill to work with others or to supervise under this orientation. In a particular situation, the behavior of the other individual may be a complete obstruction to the use of your chosen approach. In situations like these, you have no choice but to move into a backup strategy until you see an opportunity to return to the dominant style that you have found to be soundest.

Asking Your Boss

If you are now working as a secretary, you can also do this kind of data gathering about yourself by giving this book to your boss. He undoubtedly knows you well, in terms of your typical on-the-job behavior. Ask your boss to read the book and then to return to Chapter 2, picking out elements that are most typical of you. You learn a great deal about yourself by seeing yourself through your boss's eyes. Incidentally, you may find that this has a very good effect on your boss and on your work. Many bosses and secretaries have found the Grid useful in analyzing how they influence one another and in determining how to work more effectively together. The importance of realistic expectations regarding fulfilling responsibilities and working together successfully and harmoniously is equally clear to both boss and secretary, and both search for ways of creating valid expectations as the basis for decisions and action. These reciprocal attitudes make participation and involvement a natural basis for teamwork, with each able to benefit from the contributions made by the other.

Appendix
Technical Considerations Behind the Secretary-Boss Grid

This appendix is for those readers who wish to explore more fully the concept formation on which the Grid is based and to compare it with other behavioral science approaches. Researchers and theorists on behavior have taken positions on the organizationally critical quesiton, "Is there one most effective human relationship between boss and subordinate (boss and secretary), or does it depend on the situation?"

Fiedler concludes, "Match the leader's skills to properties in the situation." Hersey and Blanchard prescribe different styles for different subordinates, depending on the subordinate's maturity. Korman's resounding conclusion from reviewing the 1960s research is that there is "no conclusion possible as to what constitutes sound leadership." More recently Hunt has sought to bury the controversy through stamping the idea of one best approach as a myth, and Nystrom has apparently spoken the benediction.

This appeared as an article entitled "A Comparative Analysis of Situationalism and 9,9 Management by Principle," by Robert Blake and Jane Mouton, in the spring 1982 issue of *Organizational Dynamics*. © 1982 by AMACOM, a division of American Management Associations. Reproduced by permission. All rights reserved. The article was written from the point of view of the boss or manager. However, the underlying principles of both the Managerial Grid and the Secretary Grid are the same, so this appendix should be informative to secretary and boss alike.

Likert pondered his research and asserted, in diametric disagreement, that System 4 is the best way to exercise sound direction. McGregor's "Theory Y" is widely proclaimed as the best style. Argyris's research defends Model 2, while we interpret Grid research and conclude: "The 9,9 orientation, based as it is on principles of behavior emerging from the behavioral sciences, leads to productivity, satisfaction, creativity, and health."

The Situational or Contingency Approach

Among the approaches that are most widely used in studying situationalism are variations on the two-variable leadership model introduced by Hemphill and by Fleishman. Reddin, House, and Hersey and Blanchard have expanded on the two-variable model in several ways. From a conceptual point of view each of these authors treats the *task* and the *relationship* variables as independent of each other. Therefore, any magnitude in one can be added to or subtracted from any amount in the other. When translated into nine-point continua, the exercise of leadership might be high on the *task* variable (nine units of magnitude) and low on the *relationship* variable (one unit). Thus the boss who exercises nine units of control by structuring how the task is to be performed and adds a minimum, or one unit, of socioemotional support, is represented by $9 + 1$. This is an arithmetic basis of combining quantities from two variables. Another combination is the high control over task direction coupled with a high amount of socioemotional support that is equivalent to $9 + 9$ (high + high), or *paternalism/maternalism.* Other combinations include low task plus high relationships $(1 + 9)$ and low task plus low relationships $(1 + 1)$. The manner in which effective leadership is exercised in these contingency models is said to be dependent upon variables in the situation. For purposes of illustrating situationalism, we use Hersey and Blanchard's approach, which presumes that style should vary with the subordinate's maturity level; style is calibrated at any one of four levels. At the lowest level, M_1, the subordinate is unwilling and unable to perform; at the highest level, M_4, he or she is both willing and able to perform the task; and M_2 and M_3 are intermediate levels of maturity.

The "One Most Effective Style" Approach

The opposite interpretation leads to a different character of research and to a different practice. It also has a long history in the modern behavioral sciences, particularly in the work of Lewin, Lippitt and White, Argyris, McGregor, Likert, and the authors. These contributions served as one basis for the development of the Grid, which provides a conceptual analysis of leadership within a two-variable framework, and which we will use to illustrate the formulation that suggests the conclusion that there is one most effective style. This approach also culminates in descriptions of behavior, but the variables of the Managerial Grid are *attitudinal* and *conceptual,* with *behavior* descriptions derived from and connected with the thinking that lies behind action. On the Grid (see Figure 3) the horizontal axis represents concern for production. *Concern for* designates the character of the thinking and feeling applied to achieve any designated result in contrast to the directive of behavioral control described by situationalists. The vertical axis, *concern for people,* reflects the character of thinking and feeling as applied to people. Because a boss's actual behavior and conduct can be predicted from knowledge of how he or she thinks about achieving production with and through people, the Grid provides a more comprehensive framework for analyzing leadership theory than the situational approach.

It is important to understand that these Grid variables are conceptualized as *interdependent* with one another in the sense that it is impossible to exercise leadership without both people and tasks. These two variables are uncorrelated. Interdepen-

dence between the two dimensions is designated not by a plus
(+) but by a comma (,), as is true in systems using Cartesian
coordinates.

At the root of the interdependence issue is the following.
There is no way to exercise leadership unless both task and
people are present simultaneously. They cannot be split and
separated, each being analyzed separately without regard for
the other and then being brought into some kind of combination. A person can work on a task by doing it all alone. Alternatively, a person can have social relations during which time is
spent with others talking about the weather or who just got
divorced or the inevitability of taxes. That's chitchat. It leads
nowhere.

The importance of an interaction between interdependent
but uncorrelated variables (,) and an arithmetic coupling of
independent variables (+) cannot be overestimated because the
conceptual analysis begins at this point.

This important difference in concept formation is found in
many fields. An example from chemistry illustrates the critical
distinction between an arithmetic coupling (+) of independent
but uncorrelated variables and an interaction of interdependent
but uncorrelated variables (,). A chemical mixture is analogous
to the arithmetic combination of variables exemplified in the
Fleishman model. In a chemical mixture, such as smog, each
element in the combination retains its distinctive features. The
particles and gases that compose smog retain their unique
identities even when combined.

The mixture analogy depicts how "task" and "relationship"
each retain their distinctive character when arithmetically combined. For example, a "9" amount of task behavior is revealed in
structuring the subordinate's activities by telling him or her the
what, how, when, and where aspects in a "complete" way. A "9"
amount of socioemotional support is evidenced in the giving of
rewards, compliments, and strokes. Task direction and socioemotional support are two independent behaviors. Concep-

tually, 9 units of "direction" retain the same character whether combined with 1 unit (9 + 1) or with 9 units (9 + 9) of socio-emotional support.

By comparison, the Grid parallels a chemical compound in which variables interact with one another. In the interactive combination of chemical elements, the separate components lose their individual identities in the chemical compound produced. Water, the compound composed of hydrogen and oxygen (H_2O), has a very different character than those of the gaseous elements that make it up.

The importance of the compound concept can be demonstrated by analyzing the difference between the 1,9 and the 9,9 Grid styles by reference to what the second 9 represents in each of these two contexts. In each case, the second 9 (9,9 or 1,9) represents the same magnitude of "high concern for people." However, the 9 of "high concern for people" in the context of high concern for production, the 9,9 orientation, represents a very different way of leadership thinking and behaving than in the context of low concern for production, the 1,9 orientation. In the 9,9-oriented Grid style, the second 9 combines with the first through behavior that elicits joint effort in task definition, teamwork characterized by openness, respect, and involvement, resolution of conflict through confrontation in the interest of achieving shared agreement, and mutual commitment to productive outcomes, all combined with learning that is based on the use of critique and feedback. In the 1,9-oriented Grid style, the second 9 combines with the first to produce behavior that is characterized by warmth and friendliness in which a person yields his or her convictions for the sake of harmony, disregarding adverse impact on results and without using critique or feedback for learning. Although both 9s signify the same magnitude of concern, qualitative differences in thought, feeling, and behavior are evidenced in the compounds resulting from the interaction.

The 9,9 and comparable orientations, that is, Theory Y,

Model II, System 4, in the relationship between a boss and subordinate(s) are congruent with emerging behavioral science principles of behavior. The effort to achieve production with and through others is based on participation to gain involvement, earned commitment, mutual goal setting, creativity, two-way communication, candor, mutual trust and respect, and the resolution of differences through confrontation at *all* maturity levels. This is the most effective style; what changes with the situation is the *tactics* of its application.

From an overview perspective, these two approaches—situationalism and the "one most effective style"—define opposite directions both in theory and practice: in concept formation, development of theory, and research; and as the basis for the practice of leadership.

When instruments for measuring situational aspects are examined, it is found that the "one most effective style" alternative is not provided as one of the available options for dealing with the situation. Therefore, when measuring instruments exclude the one most effective style from comparative analysis, it is impossible to conclude that there is one most effective style. In addition, when the 9,9-oriented alternative is added to a typical situational instrument, it is judged by experienced managers to be a significantly more effective basis for dealing with a variety of situations than is the situational leadership model prescription (Blake and Mouton, 1982a).

Thus the majority of the experienced managers chose as the most effective way of exercising leadership a method unavailable to them within the situational leadership model. These results are replicated with 36 M.D. and Ph.D. mental health administrators and 38 Ph.D. and M.D. academic administrators. That these results are not unique to the United States has been demonstrated in the same study with experienced managers from other countries as well: Australia, Brazil, Japan, Malaysia, Pakistan, The Philippines, Uruguay, and Venezuela (Blake and Mouton, 1982b).

the company and says, "You've given *me* a great day's work." He also confuses himself with the company when this is followed by his using company time as though he personally owned it, giving it as a reward to the subordinate for compliant behavior.

The (+) basis of concept formation eliminates the possibility of deriving and describing the teamwork of 9,9 orientation. There is no basis for including a 9,9 alternative within the Hersey and Blanchard model because there is no possibility of a 9,9 orientation. The exclusion of the 9,9 orientation is a logical consequence of faulty theory construction.

The same character of paternalism/maternalism is embedded in the Fleishman instruments and can be seen by juxtaposing items that measure a 9 on the Initiating Structure side against items that measure a 9 on the consideration side.

For a person to score in the high-high or 9 + 9 quadrant, he or she would have to simultaneously agree to statements such as those below.

Initiating Structure		Consideration
Always rule with an iron hand	[but]	Often do favors for persons under you
Encourage after-duty work by persons of your unit a great deal	[but]	Often help persons under you with their personal problems

The boss who rules with an iron hand exercises strong control characterized as high Initiating Structure. By doing favors, he or she is demonstrating a high degree of consideration. Scoring high on both reveals a paternalistic/maternalistic orientation. The same applies for the second two sets of statements. Encouraging after-duty work is an exercise of control over the subordinate's free time and involves a high degree of work structure. If this and "Often help persons under you with personal problems" score high, we have another example of paternalistic/maternalistic supervision.

The Appeal of Paternalism/Maternalism

Reports have shown that paternalism/maternalism lacks appeal in the sense that it is not preferred as a style, nor is it found to be effective in stimulating productivity.

Despite this, paternalism/maternalism is so commonplace that it is taken at face value. The assumptions of a reciprocal relationship between reward and compliance are so deep that the test makers themselves are unaware of them. The Fleishman model is based on them, but this is not revealed in any of Fleishman's writings, nor is it recognized as such by his supporters or critics. The same can be said for Hersey and Blanchard. Nowhere do they acknowledge that paternalism/maternalism is inherent in their theory and test construction; yet it is recommended as the basis of supervision, particularly in the linking of reward to obedience.

We offer the following to aid in understanding why the appeal of this approach has been so substantial. Paternalistic/maternalistic practices of child rearing are based on the (+) mode of concept formation with rewards exchanged for compliance. ("Clean your plate and you can have dessert," for example.) This way of exercising control over children is widespread; many have come to accept it as second nature without deliberately thinking about it or critically examining the assumptions embedded within it. Among adults, the model is retained, also without critical examination or deliberate thought, as natural, appropriate, and sound, particularly when compared with the 9,1, 5,5, or 1,9 orientations, and in the absence of a deeper understanding of the 9,9 orientation. Though it is demanding, paternalism/maternalism does in fact reward compliance.

Research on Situationalism

It is not surprising the consistently inconclusive results have been found in studies where measuring instruments were based on a 9+9 paternalistic/maternalistic mode of concept formation. Korman brought together research on the (+) basis of concept formation in the Fleishman model and associated measuring instruments that had been published up to 1966. No consistently positive correlations are found in 26 studies that sought to connect the paternalistic leadership style and effectiveness. Larson, Hunt, and Osborn—and more recently Nystrom—have carried the (+) concept formation to its logical conclusion, but appear unaware of the hidden assumptions to which they have committed themselves. Accepting the concept formation embedded within the Fleishman instruments as given, they conclude that "the desirability of the preferred high + high (9 + 9) style is a myth." Failing to recognize the differences between 9 + 9 and 9,9, they imply that they are rejecting 9,9 while, in fact, they are correctly rejecting the conclusion that 9 + 9 (paternalism/maternalism) is indeed an invalid basis for the practice of effective leadership. Because the measuring instruments used in these studies are based on the (+) rather than the (,) concept, the conclusions drawn have nothing to do with evaluating Theory Y, Model II, System 4, or 9,9. The most valid and appropriate conclusion from these sources of evidence is: When the 9,9 orientation, Theory Y, or other criterion is omitted from the measuring system, no "one most effective" style of leadership is consistently better than any other style.

9,9 Orientation

By comparison, the style revealed in the 9,9 orientation is significantly different from 9 + 9 paternalism/maternalism. The boss in the following dialogue is exercising leadership in the same situation as that described earlier, but this time from a 9,9 orientation.

Boss: You've read the shift book. It's pretty dull, but you need to get it all done.
Subordinate: I'll do my best.
Boss: Instead of making the seven adjustments on each of the three machines, a machine at a time,

I want you to make the same adjustment on each machine one at a time in sequence. Start with balancing the rotes on all three. Then come back to the first machine and replace the belt. Repeat that on machines 2 and 3, and so forth. Does that make sense?

Subordinate: But boss, that's ineffecient. It's really better to deal with all seven adjustments on machine 1 and then to work on machine 2.

Boss: I appreciate your suggestion, Joe. I know they have nothing to complain about, but I can't prove that to the operators. It's one of those trust and confidence problems between two departments. This way I can personally guarantee them that each one of the adjustments was completed.

Subordinate: Well, if there's a problem with guaranteeing them, let's solve it, but in a way that permits me to work in a sound manner.

Boss: Yes, you're right. I suppose we could. . . .

Subordinate: We could. It's true that anyone might miss an adjustment or two working down through one machine. You see something that needs fixing and it captures your attention, interrupts an orderly sequence . . . I've a checklist in my mind anyway, but I could put it on paper and check off each item as I complete it. That way you could offer them the same assurance of quality but without my losing efficiency.

Boss: Of course. Give me a ring thirty minutes before quitting time to let me know your progress.

Subordinate: Okay.

Boss: *(answering phone some hours later)* Yeah, yeah, Joe. What . . .?

Subordinate:	I've almost got it all done. I'll get through by quitting time.
Boss:	That's good. How did the checklist work?
Subordinate:	No problem. Really a good idea. I'm convinced that I skipped over nothing.

Here we see the same situation managed in a 9,9-oriented way. The boss acknowledges the subordinate's disagreement and is open to a reexamination of what he had in mind. Joe's proposal seemed to have merit and the addition of a checklist leads to a course of action that is jointly agreed upon as sounder. The approach he has expressed is centered on the subordinate's impact on the work itself. Here we see the result of using open participation, of candor, of conflict solution based on respect for differences and exploring alternatives and possibilities, and the effects of these on involvement and commitment, mutual goal setting, and so on.

Comparing a 9,9 Orientation with Other Styles

These descriptions of two different ways of supervising a machine operator have been evaluated by more than 100 managers of all levels and from a number of different organizations, but before they had heard any professional presentation of the leadership assumptions embedded in each. To a statistically significant degree, managers preferred the 9,9 orientation as a way of exercising leadership—evaluating it from the subordinate's perspective as more involving, earning greater commitment, and stimulating greater creativity—and as a sounder basis for achieving production. In spite of these differences that lead to the conclusion that the 9,9 orientation is a sounder basis of supervision than is paternalism/maternalism, we find a different result when participants rate responsibility and satisfaction felt by each supervisor. No statistically significant differences were found between the supervisor's feelings of responsibility and satisfaction in the two situations. This lends support to the appeal of paternalism/maternalism; that is, the supervisor feels that a paternalistic/maternalistic style of supervision provides him or her with a high degree of responsibility and satisfaction.

Where measuring instruments are designed on the basis of interacting variables, research findings demonstrate significant generalizations as to the one most effective leadership style. One series of studies at the Institute of Social Research of the University of Michigan reveals both a statistical and a direct experimental nature. The statistical evidence can be interpreted in the following way: The closer a work group's leadership style is to System 4, the higher the productivity. System 4 is based on a (,) and approximates a 9,9 orientation. This conclusion has been verified in a wide range of studies involving more than 20,000 managers and 200,000 employees. The experimental aspect of the Likert work involved moving System 4 managers from high-producing units into low-producing units and evaluating changes in productivity on a before-and-after basis. The System 4 managers brought productivity to a significantly higher level than the non-System 4 managers being replaced had achieved.

Similar conclusions are drawn by Argyris from an in-depth clinical study of six company presidents. They were learning to change their behavior from Model I (approximating a 9,1 orientation) to Model II (approximating a 9,9 orientation); concurrent increases in profitability were reported as the change took place.

Another line of research relates to Grid Organization Development. A summary of studies in which the impact of a 9,9 orientation on a variety of performance criteria has been evaluated demonstrates consistently positive results. One of the most important of these was longitudinal in character and permitted before-and-after comparisons of two subsidiaries of the same parent company. Both subsidiaries operated in comparable markets, distributed under the same brand names, gained access to new products at the same time, gained similar advantages from headquarters Research and Development, and competed with each other for the same corporate financial dollar for growth, development, and expansion. One subsidiary was engaged in Grid Organization Development, and the matched control was not. A ten-year comparison based on annual reports led to the conclusion that the Grid-active company increased its profitability over the matched control by 400 percent. Other studies concerned with specifics show a 100 percent reduction in nonscheduled overtime, a 67 percent reduction in monthly outlay for small tools, a 50 percent reduction in hourly cost of maintenance, and so forth.

The relationship between career success and Grid style has also been the subject of major research. Correcting for age differences, two independent investigations demonstrate that managers who advance higher on the career ladder are more likely to have a 9,9 orientation than are those who do not. One of these investigations is based on a study of 716 managers in one company as presented by the authors. The replication is based on 731 managers from many different companies in a study by Hall.

A high degree of consistency is evident in this survey of industrial and other research. Apparently a 9,9 type of leadership orientation results in more productive outcomes than any other basis for dealing with subordinates, clients, students, and so forth. We conclude that the conceptual basis for combining variables is at the origin of the controversy. The regrouping of research in terms of whether it uses measuring instruments of the additive (+) or interactive (,) types provides another basis for resolving this controversy. The soundest basis for combining variables is by compounding (,) rather than by adding (+) them. The (+) basis of grouping brings together studies that fail to include the "one most effective style" as a variable, and this basis produces inconsistent results. The (,) includes the "one most effective style" and produces positive correlations between productivity and a 9,9 leadership style. The most plausible conclusion is that when it is included in comparative research, the 9,9 orientation is found to be the most effective way of leading.

Why the Appeal of Situationalism?

We need to understand why a family of ideas under the rubric of situationalism (that is, hopscotch situationalism, paternalism/ maternalism as the high + high condition, and so forth) has become popular in spite of the fact that research evidence fails to support it and scientific formulations run counter to it.

There are several possible answers.

One answer is related to the times in which we live—this "do you own thing" era. This comes to mean freedom—freedom from principle, whether biological, psychological, or social. This freedom is possibly confused with freedom from moral impera- tives, with roots in the history of religion. Yet it is a rejection of inherent order in the sense that one's personal will replaces scientific order with respect to drugs, child rearing, or exercising organizational leadership.

A second answer comes from sheer frustration with complex- ity, which leads to a desire for simplicity. Principles of behavior are complex, difficult to learn, and more difficult to practice. Acting without principle is less demanding and has its own rewards in the sense that the sole criterion is likely to be short term. Rewards are geared to this sense of the "immediate." Actions based on principles are longer term, slower to come into being, and possible only when a person is prepared to take the longer view. When "a day at a time" rather than "this year and next" is the criterion for measuring action, the time horizon for management by principles is simply not available.

A third answer is reliance on common sense. Life experiences are not to be disregarded as a source of emotional validity. If they lead to conclusions that run counter to scientific analysis, reliance is placed on personal experience and subjective "right- ness" over science. In other words, if everybody is doing it and it "feels good," that's evidence enough.

A fourth answer relates to childhood experiences in which

parents may have provided their children with no consistent model; instead, they shifted from one style to another—expressing personal gratification at one time, frustration at another, indifference at some other time, and the desire to reduce tensions through accommodation at other times—and consequently the child was unable to identify any pattern to their behavior. When he or she reaches adulthood, the child, therefore, has developed a managerial value system that validates backing off, backing and filling, pushing, or responding with sweetness and light. All are appropriate, depending on the situation. It is natural under these conditions to be flexible and inconsistent without experiencing internal contradiction.

Another explanation for the appeal of situationalism is that the leader wants to maintain a maximum freedom from commitments. He or she wants to maneuver at will, keeping all options open, and in this way avoid the obligation to strive to apply principles to his or her supervision. A situationally oriented leader, who is unpredictable to subordinates and colleagues alike, can use this unpredictability to maximize his or her power. When others have no basis for anticipation, the person who exercises leadership creates no obligations of constancy.

In a similar way, situationalism may appeal to the training and development professional—that is, he or she is unlikely to be challenged on what he or she may feel is an impregnable position: "If you advocate nothing, but leave the issue open and up in the air, how can you be criticized?" Or "If you present all the options and let the person choose, you have given the other person the freedom of choice."

These different explanations may account for the slow emergence of a shift from a common-sense empiricism to management by principles (9,9 orientation) on the world scene.

Resolutions That Fail to Solve the Controversy

A controversy between two fundamental positions of such importance as these for sound management and organization development can be expected to spawn any number of resolutions.

The reactions to this research among those who previously preferred situationalism are important as a study in themselves. A cognitive dissonance is created. Their feelings and emotions lead them in one direction, but theory and research lead them in the opposite direction. The interesting question then is, "How do they go about relieving this dissonance?" There are three possibilities. One is to shift and embrace the evidence of research. A second is to reject the evidence out of hand. Neither of these is common.

The third and most common reaction is to search for some way to retain their predisposition while they simultaneously accept the research conclusions. The most common adaptation seems to be predicated on the notion that the two theories are somehow equal but different and, therefore, both can be embraced simultaneously. We have identified a large number of different ways by which those with a situational predisposition attempt to retain their convictions and yet come to terms with research findings that contradict them.

None provides for a satisfactory resolution. We have observed people experiencing these reactions, recognizing the inherent fallacies in them, and then doing one of two things: either shifting to another rationalization or, more commonly, acknowledging the evidence from the research and beginning to assess the implications of shifting toward the "most effective style" viewpoints. Following are explanations intended to resolve the contradiction, yet each fails to achieve that purpose.

Short Term vs. Long Term

One is: "Situationalism is for the short term—on the way to one most effective style for the longer term." This solution permits retention of both positions as "equal but different." Translated into Grid terms it says, "use 9,1 or 1,9 or 1,1 or 5,5 or paternalism, or whatever seems to fit the situation in the short term, as you seek to move toward the 9,9 orientation—which is more appropriate at later maturity stages."

The internal reasoning of this argument is itself contradictory, as it remains to be demonstrated that the 9,9 orientation can be achieved in the long term by the use of 9,9 or other orientations in the short term.

Attitude vs. Behavior

"The two theories are both feasible because they account for different kinds of behavior." Grid is thinking and attitude. Situationalism is real behavior. Alluded to elsewhere as a failure of the critic to understand that the Grid is both thinking and attitude on the one hand and behavior on the other, this explanation creates a difference that does not exist.

A 9,9 Orientation as the Underlying Motivation of Situational Leadership Styles

Another allied basis for relieving the controversy is, "You can have a 9,9-oriented attitude with any situational leadership style." The contradiction is that a 9,9 orientation at the attitudinal level is incompatible with one-way communication, withholding rationale, and directing the subordinate as to who, when, where, and so forth, while withholding socioemotional support, all at the behavioral level. All of these behaviors are compatible with the 9,1, not the 9,9, orientation, and all are consistent with prescriptions for dealing with the subordinate at the M_1 level of maturity. The argument, therefore, is without substance.

Use of the 9,9 Orientation as an Alternative Within Situationalism

Still another attempted solution is this: "Situationalism is big enough to include 9,9—whenever it fits." This approach retains the logic of situationalism and merely adds the 9,9 orientation to the medley of possibilities, acknowledging that sometimes (but only sometimes) the 9,9 orientation makes the best fit. This resolution simply incorporates 9,9 into an expanded version of situationalism. It already has been analyzed as hopscotch situationalism (statistical 5,5) and found deficient on a number of grounds.

View of Both as Having the Same Emphasis

Other authors relieve this tension by drawing a moral that obscures the issue. "Despite the unresolved controversy, one useful and important point emerges: Leaders need to consider the relationship needs of their subordinates as well as the demands of the task at hand." This statement, itself based on the (+) way of thinking, appears to resolve the difference while maintaining a hands-off attitude toward the status quo.

Principles vs. Behavior

Another reaction that makes it unnecessary to face the deeper issue is this: "Even though you apply the same principles at all maturity levels, you still have to shift techniques with subordinates at different maturity levels. You're still dealing with situationalism, right?"

Situationalism is *not* engineered to principles of the 9,9 sort. Leadership action is determined by subordinate readiness and a set of presumptive rules that are not geared to principles. It is coincidental when prescribed action and a principle of behavior are congruent.

Differences Between Different Leaders

"Different leaders are effective, but speak differently. Look at World War II leaders—Eisenhower and Patton, for instance. Two more different styles would be harder to find. How can you say there is one most effective style in the face of such evidence?" This argument looks at surface differences and may obscure deeper likenesses, while at the same time hiding real differences that may have reduced each leader's effectiveness from what might otherwise have been sounder leadership. Patton's slapping a GI is no particular compliment to his leadership effectiveness.

Unilateral Directions Treated as Equivalent to Goal Setting

According to the situational leadership model, an M_1 subordinate ought to be told what to do and two-way communication should be kept to a minimum. On the other hand, the Grid theory holds that goal setting is the best way to relate to an M_1 subordinate. Any difference, really? This approach to eliminating a difference by making alternative approaches appear equal obscures an important difference between the two.

Telling someone what do do, where, when, and how, with little or no give-and-take, creates a reactive, dependent (or resistant) attitude on the subordinate's part. Sooner or later this leads to resentment, anger, and antagonism. By comparison, mutual goal setting promotes participation, involvement, and thinking about how to reach the goals. Mutual goal setting stimulates a proactive attitude, a readiness for give-and-take, and a positive attitude toward learning. We see, therefore, that telling subordinates what to do and mutual goal setting are very different ways of supervising. To treat them as different but equal is to obscure issues of importance to stimulating sound involvement, positive learning, and effective performance.

Biased Investigators

"Investigators have been advocating one most effective style for years. I expect dedicated situationalists could design research or even reinterpret these data to support their point of view." Empirical research is always subject to reinterpretation and verification.

Belief in Situationalism

"I don't care what the research shows, I'm committed to situationalism." This reaction is consistent with the paternalistic orientation, the result being that subjective validity is accorded to situationalism in disregard of conceptual logic and objective research.

Yes, . . . Reality Being What It Is . . .

"The logic and evidence for a most effective style is persuasive, but the size of the real-life problem is staggering; it's overwhelming. The only practical solution is to manage situationally." This pessimistic reaction takes the status quo as given and rejects the likelihood that change can be induced.

Though each reaction tries to accommodate to the cognitive dissonance produced by incompatible theories, none of these armchair solutions resolves the problem by grappling with its cause: two logics of concept formation, of which only one can be regarded as valid in the light of earlier-cited research.

Reactions to this research by those predisposed toward the 9,9 orientation are positive probably because these findings support preexisting solutions. They lift the confusion that has come to prevail in this area and reinforce conclusions already reached.

Implications for a Science of Behavior

A value of science rests in its ability to discover "regularities" in phenomena and to make explicit the underlying principles that govern their behavior. Principles of physics allow engineers to act with confidence and authority in dealing with the atom as an energy source. Surgeons work with biological principles when performing open heart surgery. Situationalism is comparable with the practice of engineering carried out independently of principles of physics, or surgery performed disregarding the principles of biology. By analogy, emerging behavioral science principles are consistently employed in the same manner as the physical science principles that underlie the practice of engineering, regardless of the particular situation—whether constructing a building, bridge, or boat—to which the engineering effort is applied. Principles that govern human behavior to the extent that they provide for predictability are emerging from the behavioral sciences, and practitioners are learning to apply these in concrete situations. The effective exercise of leadership can now be based on emerging behavioral science principles.

There are ten major emerging principles of human behavior that seem critical to effectiveness. These are subject to refinement and revision based on future research, and are provided here by way of illustration of possibilities rather than as final formulations. These principles are summarized in Table 1. The science of behavior can be expected to incorporate these constant principles and to provide a tactical basis for utilizing them consistently across situations.

Shared participation, for example, is a practice that can consistently produce favorable results in terms of utilization of human resources. Promoting open participation at all maturity levels allows those involved to exercise mutual influence on outcomes and to contribute to job effectiveness as well as satisfaction. Under a 9,9 Grid orientation, it is possible for this kind of participation to be constant across maturity levels. By comparison, the situational model concept of participation is that of a technique useful as a socioemotional reward to promote greater willingness to obey.

Resolution of differences and conflicts is prerequisite to understanding and agreement for behavior based on principles. No method of addressing conflicts is discussed in the situational model, yet unresolved conflicts may undermine sound relationships. The soundest approach to conflict resolution is confrontation, an integral element of the 9,9 orientation.

Individual change is a key issue in effectiveness, and its facilitation is viewed in at least two significantly different ways. In the situational model, change is based on Pavlovian connections between stimulus, response, and rewards, as extended and refined by Skinner and others. This way of inducing change has demonstrated usefulness as the basis for predicting animal learning and for controlling people with limited mental functioning. Choice based on personal insight and conviction is eliminated or restricted when some external agent extends or

Table 1. The extent to which behavioral science principles are embedded within management by principle (9,9 orientation) and situational leadership theory.

Principles	Key Words	Situational Leadership Theory	Management by Principles
1. Fulfillment through participation is the motivation that gives character to human activity and supports productivity.	Participation.	A technique used as socioemotional reward for compliance at intermediate maturity levels only.	Skill in the use of interdependent interaction process is basic for teamwork at all maturity levels.
2. Open communication is essential for the exercise of self- and shared responsibility.	Candor.	Not mentioned.	Prerequisite to effective participation.
3. Accepting others as capable of reaching standards of excellence promotes trust and respect.	Trust and respect.	Helpful for delegation at fourth level of maturity only.	Essential for shared participation.
4. Shared participation in problem solving and decision making stimulates active involvement and commitment, productivity, and creative thinking.	Involvement and commitment.	Boss-controlled and permitted at third level of maturity only.	Core motivation underlying learning, problem solving, and production at all maturity levels.

5. Conflicts are solved by direct confrontation, and with understanding and agreement as the basis of cooperative effort.	Conflict resolution.	Not dealt with because subordinates are expected to comply.	Open confrontation and resolution of differences essential for shared understanding and agreement.
6. Mutual agreement is the strongest basis for supervision.	Consensus.	Irrelevant since subordinates are expected to obey at lower levels or to exercise self-direction at higher levels of maturity.	A shared value that may not always be achievable.
7. Effective interaction between boss and subordinate enhances synergy.	Synergy.	Not mentioned.	Human resources utilization based on teamwork.
8. Management is by objectives.	Goals and objectives.	Set by the boss for subordinates with some subordinate input permitted at higher maturity levels.	Mutually set as the basis for organization and direction of work.
9. Organization members who cooperate are interdependent on mutual support.	Mutual support.	Not considered as an aspect of management.	A result of team-based interdependence.
10. Learning from work experience is through critique and feedback.	Change and development.	Reinforcement of subordinate compliance through giving or withholding of socioemotional rewards. Feedback disregarded or rarely mentioned.	Use of open critique and single and double feedback for analyzing experience and increasing insight, understanding, and effectiveness.

withholds rewards in exchange for compliance. Extrinsic rewards are far less sound as the basis for motivating effort than are intrinsic rewards—that is, satisfaction derived from doing the job well.

The Hersey-Blanchard theory is also contradicted by the vast majority of psychological research and clinical evidence in terms of dealing with children at the M_1 level of maturity. Applications of cybernetic learning theory, for example, tell us that mistakes are important elements of acquiring understanding or skill. Feeling free to experiment, which means risking mistakes, is most possible when a climate of support is present; otherwise, a learner is reluctant to try for fear a mistake will bring correction or result in withdrawal of support, as is prescribed in the Hersey and Blanchard situational model. A cybernetic model of learning, as described by Wiener and Ashby, including single- and double-loop learning, is far more pertinent when applied in the context of healthy young people with adults, regardless of maturity level. In other words, the two approaches are radically different with respect to approaches to change and development.

The whole issue of extending or withholding support, when viewed from the perspective of the broader research field, particularly with respect to research on child-rearing practices, leads to the conclusion that withholding of socioemotional support is one of the more devastating aspects in child rearing and when this occurs in the extreme, the psychological injuries are permanent. A host of clinical experts emphasize the importance of unconditional positive regard in any undertaking with another person, regardless of maturity level, which means responding to the other person's feelings and emotions in a constructive and positive manner.

Withholding socioemotional support until compliance is forthcoming is in the opposite direction from each of these sources of evidence that point to the importance of creating a learning environment through creating a positive socioemotional support system. Additional examples of successful implementation of the principles listed in Table 1 are available elsewhere.

A summary of these differences in the application of principles can be seen by comparing Figure 5 with Figure 6. Figure 5 shows us that under situationalism actual leadership style shifts with the maturity of the subordinate. Figure 6 shows us that actual leadership style remains consistent without regard to the subordinate's maturity level under a management-by-principles approach.

From an everyday perspective, it might be thought that a kernel of truth is embedded within situationalism. This relates

Figure   5. Subordinates at each level of maturity are dealt with in a different style.

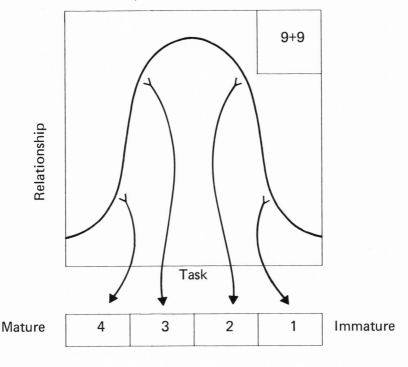

Figure 6. Subordinates at all levels of maturity are dealt with in a 9,9-oriented way.

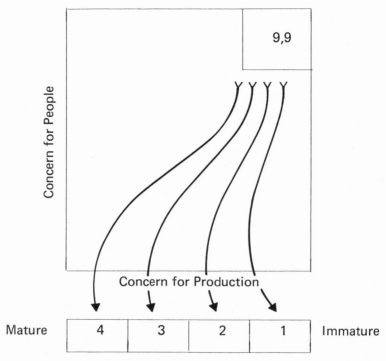

to the observation that because no two situations are alike, it therefore follows that each must be managed differently. Unfortunately this solution also precludes management by principles. The resolution must retain management by principles across situations while applying them in ways appropriate to circumstances. This leads to the distinction between principles themselves and the tactics of their application.

Figure 7 shows how the principle of goal setting is constant at all maturity levels, and yet the tactics of application differ. With an M_1 subordinate, for example, goals set are near term and easy to reach, with clear pathways to their accomplishment and with immediate feedback as to progress. With an M_4 subordi-

Figure 7. Goal setting remains 9,9-oriented, although some tactics vary according to subordinates' maturity levels.

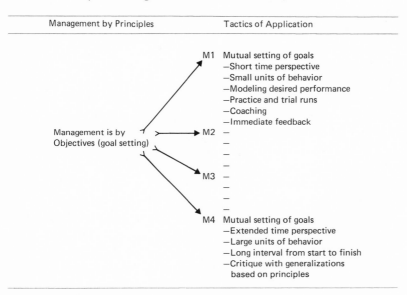

Management by Principles	Tactics of Application
	M1 Mutual setting of goals —Short time perspective —Small units of behavior —Modeling desired performance —Practice and trial runs —Coaching —Immediate feedback
Management is by Objectives (goal setting)	**M2** — — — —
	M3 — — —
	M4 Mutual setting of goals —Extended time perspective —Large units of behavior —Long interval from start to finish —Critique with generalizations based on principles

nate, mutually set goals are complex, subtle, and of such character as to make it impractical to do more than broadly outline pathways toward their accomplishment and set intermediate critique points for their achievement and the evaluation of progress. Goal setting is a constant principle from M_1 to M_4. Tactics of goal setting shift with the circumstances.

Given the central importance of principles within the 9,9 orientation and the relative absence of principles orientation in the situational model, it now becomes possible to explain why situational theorists have advocated the concept of flexibility so forcibly and why "one most effective style" theorists have concentrated attention on versatility. Flexibility is empirically determined by the situation. It is unprincipled. This fact explains why many have been reluctant to go along with situationalism but have not known the reasons for their reluctance. Versatility, on the other hand, identifies a talent for being able to apply principles consistently but in a tactically sound manner and in a way that brings about effective results regardless of maturity level and other presumably important aspects of situations.

McGregor concluded, and we agree, that when a manager understands Theory Y (that is, the 9,9 orientation) as a way of managing people, then "the tactics are worked out in the light of circumstances. . . . The manager . . . will invent his own tactics provided he has a conception of the strategy involved."

Summary

Two fundamentally different approaches to theory, research, and practice point in opposite and mutually contradictory directions. Because both cannot be valid, a controversy has arisen as to whether behavior should be conceived of as being contingent upon the situation or whether there is one most effective style for all situations. In the first case, the leader changes behavior to fit the situation. In the second, the leader changes the situation to bring it into line with sound principles of behavior as these are emerging in the behavioral sciences.

We have examined the roots of this controversy and the widely unexamined assumptions embedded within the conceptual structure supporting each side of it. Several interrelated kinds of evidence have been presented that lead to the conclusion that one best style is a sounder basis for the exercise of effective cooperation. These include the following:

Explanations for the absence of the "one most effective style" alternative are based on an examination of the situational theories from which the measurement practices are derived. This leads to the conclusion that the explanation lies in the manner in which task and relationship variables are combined. Following Fleishman and Reddin, the Hersey and Blanchard situational model is predicated on an additive (+) basis of combining independent variables that produces a mixture. This basis of separating two variables and treating them as though independent of each other loses the concept of leadership and creates several of the unfortunate consequences of reductionism. When high magnitudes of both variables are present, the result is $9+9$ (high-high) or paternalism/maternalism. By comparison, "one best style" models are based on interaction between two interdependent but uncorrelated variables that results in a shift in the character of leadership. This is designated by a (,) basis of compounding that identifies and defines the 9,9 orientation. The important distinction is at the level of concept formation rather than at the level of statistical treatment, where the same terms are used. If the basic concept formation is inappropriate, no amount of sophisticated statistical analysis can rectify the difficulties inherent in the theory itself.

Published research was examined to determine whether the measuring instruments used are based on concept formation of the (+) or the (,) character. Research based on the (+) concept formation and test construction has consistently demonstrated that there is no one best style. By comparison, when concept formation and test construction of the instruments are consistent with the compounding concept (,), research conclusions have demonstrated consistently that (a) one style is most effective, and (b) this style is described by the 9,9 orientation or others essentially equivalent to it—that is, System 4, Theory Y, Model II.

The Hersey and Blanchard situational model and the Blake and Mouton Grid model were then compared to determine the manner in which each deals with behavioral science concepts. In comparison with the 9,9 Grid orientation, the situational model limits participation and conceives of it as a technique, fails to deal with conflict resolution as the basis of achieving understanding and agreement, and disregards critique and feedback as basic to learning, development, and change. The one concept relied on by Hersey and Blanchard is Skinnerian reinforcement theory; that is, the boss rewards subordinates for compliance with socioemotional support, or reduces noncompliance by coercion (Hersey and Blanchard, 1982). By comparison, reward in the "one most effective style" approach is intrinsic to open participation that promotes involvement and commitment.

Principles of behavior emerging from the behavioral sciences are interpreted as providing the strategy for conceiving the exercise of cooperation based on open participation, candor, the promotion of trust and respect, stimulation of involvement and commitment, goal setting, confrontational conflict solving, and learning through critique and feedback. These strategies do not change with situational variables, but the tactics of how they are applied shift with the maturity level of subordinates and other moderating variables.

Rationalizations that permit both theories to be simultaneously embraced were identified and discussed as examples of how incorrect thinking may be relied on to reduce cognitive dissonance.

These findings provide for the resolution of this controversy. They consistently demonstrate that the 9,9 orientation (System 4, Model II, Theory Y) is the most effective style at the level of conceptual strategy, with tactics of practice geared to situations.

This clarification makes it possible to strengthen cooperation and teamwork in its many applications within industry and government, mental health settings, and the academic world by bringing practices into alignment with sound theory of behavior.

Selected Bibliography

For a comprehensive review of the literature on situational leadership theory, see F. E. Fiedler, "A Contingency Model of Leadership Effectiveness," in L. Berkowitz (ed.), *Advances in Experimental and Social Psychology* (Academic Press, 1964), E. A. Fleishman, "Leadership Opinion Questionnaire" (Science Research Associates, Inc., 1960), E. A. Fleishman, "The Measurement of Leadership Attitudes in Industry" (*Journal of Applied Psychology*, Volume 39, 1955), E. A. Fleishman, "Twenty Years of Consideration and Structure," in E. A. Fleishman and J. G. Hunt (eds.), *Current Developments in the Study of Leadership* (Southern Illinois University Press, 1973), J. Hall, "To Achieve or Not: The Manager's Choice" (*California Management Review*, April 1976), J. K. Hemphill, "Leader Behavior Description" (*Personnel Research Board*, Ohio State University, 1950), P. G. Hersey and K. H. Blanchard, "Life Cycle Theory of Leadership" (*Training and Development Journal*, May 1969), P. G. Hersey and K. H. Blanchard, *Management of Organizational Behavior: Utilizing Human Resources* (4th ed.) (Prentice-Hall, 1982), R. J. House, "A Path-Goal Theory of Leader Effectiveness" (*Administrative Science Quarterly*, September 1971), A. K. Korman, "Consideration, 'Initiating Structure,' and Organizational Criteria—A Review" (*Personnel Psychology*, Winter 1966), L. L. Larson, J. G. Hunt, and R. N. Osborn, "The Great Hi-Hi Leader Behavior Myth: A Lesson from Occam's Razor" (*Academy of Management Journal*, December 1976), P. C. Nystrom, "Managers and the Hi-Hi Leader Myth" (*Academy of Management Journal*, June 1978), W. J. Reddin, *Managerial Effectiveness* (McGraw-Hill, 1970), and W. Schutz, "FIRO, Awareness Scales Manual" (Consulting Psychologists Press, 1978).

The "one most effective style" literature includes C. Argyris, *Increasing Leadership Effectiveness* (John Wiley & Sons, 1976), C.

187

Argyris, *Personality and Organization* (Harper Bros., 1957), R. R. Blake and J. S. Mouton, *The Managerial Grid* (Gulf Publishing, 1964), R. R. Blake and J. S. Mouton, *The New Managerial Grid* (Gulf Publishing, 1978), R. R. Blake and J. S. Mouton, *The Versatile Manager: A Grid Profile* (Dow Jones-Irwin, 1980), R. R. Blake and J. S. Mouton, "A Comparative Analysis of Situationalism and the 9,9 Approach of Management by Principle" (*Organizational Dynamics,* Spring 1982a), R. R. Blake and J. S. Mouton, "Theory and Research for Developing a Science of Leadership" (*Journal of Applied Behavioral Science,* Spring 1982b), and R. Likert, *The Human Organization: Its Management and Value* (McGraw-Hill, 1967).

Research findings conducted by Likert correlating the increase of productivity to System 4 are found in R. Likert, *The Human Organization: Its Management and Value* (McGraw-Hill, 1967), and R. G. Likert and J. G. Likert, *New Ways of Managing Conflict* (McGraw-Hill, 1976).

Similar conclusions drawn by Argyris are reviewed in C. Argyris and D. A. Schön, *Theory in Practice: Increasing Professional Effectiveness* (Jossey-Bass, 1974).

A summary of studies in which the impact of a 9,9 orientation on a variety of performance criteria has been evaluated is presented in R. R. Blake and J. S. Mouton, *The New Managerial Grid* (Gulf Publishing, 1978).

See also R. R. Blake and J. S. Mouton, *The Managerial Grid* (Gulf Publishing, 1964) for a study of the relationship between career success and Grid style. Hall also did a similar study. See J. Hall, "To Achieve or Not: The Manager's Choice" (*California Management Review,* April 1976).

Glaser's supposition that situationalism is for the short term on the way to one most effective style is presented in R. Glaser and C. Glaser, *Managing by Design* (Addison-Wesley, 1981).

Change, under the situational leadership model, is based on Pavlovian connections between stimulus, response, and reward. See B. F. Skinner, *Science and Human Behavior* (The Macmillan Company, 1953).

For applications of cybernetic learning theory, see N. Wiener, *Cybernetics: Or Control and Communication in the Animal and the Machine* (Wiley, 1948), and R. Ashby, *Design for a Brain* (Chapman & Hall, 1966).

The issue of extending or withholding support on the basis of maturity level is found in P. Mussen and N. Eisenberg-Berg, *Roots of Caring, Sharing and Helping* (W. H. Freeman, 1977), and R. Spitz, "Hospitalism: A Follow-up Report" (*Psychoanalytic Study of the Child,* Volume 2, 1946, Yale University). See also C. R. Rogers, *Counseling and Psychotherapy* (Houghton-Mifflin, 1942), and J. R. Gibb, *Trust: A New View of Personal and Organizational Development* (Guild of Tutors Press, 1978).

Goal setting as a constant principle at all maturity levels, with only the tactics of application varying, is explained in R. R. Blake and J. S. Mouton, *The Versatile Manager: A Grid Profile* (Dow Jones-Irwin, 1980). Versatility is being able to apply principles consistently but in a tactically sound manner regardless of maturity. See R. R. Blake and J. S. Mouton, *The Versatile Manager: A Grid Profile* (Dow Jones-Irwin, 1980), and D. McGregor, *The Human Side of Enterprise* (McGraw-Hill, 1960) and *The Professional Manager* (McGraw-Hill, 1967).

Index